Grandma has a "Tale"

Grandma has a "Tale"

Bernice Zakin

Copyright © 2011 by Bernice Zakin.

Library of Congress Control Number: 2011961279
ISBN: Hardcover   978-1-4653-0956-3
              Softcover   978-1-4653-0955-6
              Ebook   978-1-4653-0957-0

All rights reserved. No part of this book may be reproduced or transmitted in any form or by any means, electronic or mechanical, including photocopying, recording, or by any information storage and retrieval system, without permission in writing from the copyright owner.

This book was printed in the United States of America.

To order additional copies of this book, contact:
Xlibris Corporation
1-888-795-4274
www.Xlibris.com
Orders@Xlibris.com
108619

CONTENTS

Grandma Has A Tale 17

Grandma Ada..22

Memories 24

Way Way Back When 26

Way Back When..28

Death In The Afternoon...29

The Important Lessons Of My Life 30

Employment Enjoyment?...34

Never Pin Your Hopes Too High 35

Potsy 37

A Crack In The Sidewalk..38

On With The Memories...41

Summer Camp 43

How To Get A Job 45

Don't Be Fooled By Glitter 47

"Moving Day" In The Rental Era 49

The Woman In 8B 51

Depressing Times 53

A Really Safe Place 55

I Tried To Laugh But It Just Wasn't Funny.............................57

My Mother's Possible Advice To My 18 Year Old Self...........58

As I Recall, He Was Chubby, Etc..59

How I Got Engaged 60

Anti Semitism 62

Four Letter Words 65

My Father's Family 66

Fort Worth, Texas Also Known As Cow Town.......................74

Welcome To The World 79

Those Texan Years 81

My First Airplane Ride...82

I Remember You 84

Time Hath Wrought Changes 86

Seeing Yourself Through Someone Else's Eyes.......................87

Was I A Good Mother? 88

Eddie..90

The 5 Towns And Lido 93

The Nevers In My Life..101

I Promised To Keep It A Secret..102

A Horse Of Another Color...103

The Table Of Contents 105

The Red Leather Diary...107

They "Tripped" Up	109
Barbi And Ken	111
Telling Your Children How To Raise Their Children	113
Career Bound	114
The End Of The World	117
2nd Time Around	120
Is There Anybody Out There?	122
Ellie—Poignant Details About Her Death	123
Looking Through Old Albums And Scrap Books	124
Who Would Come To My Funeral?	126
Never Go Back	128
Ah Youth!	129
Gone But Not Forgotten	130
A Beautiful Spot—But	132
No Heat	134
The Trip Would Be Punishing	136
A Meal Surreal	138
My Inheritance	140
Bling	142
Young At Heart	143
My Quandary	144
Ny Times Obits	145
Important Notice On J Date	147

What A Great Dinner 149

Mail 151

Old Friends 153

Why Are "We" Doing This 154

I'm Never Going To Do Anything I Don't Want To Do Ever Again!....156

They Give—I Take... 158

"Time Will Tell" 160

A Medical Memory 161

Getting Lost 163

Disaster In The Closet 164

Service With A Smile? 166

A Moving Experience 168

Ladies Night Out 171

My Lovely Great Grandchildren? 174

How Old Is Old? 176

The Ups And Downs Of Life 177

The Wonderful Years 178

Really Rich 179

Things Left Undone 181

Learning To Drive 182

If I Could Do It Over Again 184

Brrr!!!! 186

Monday 8 Am This Morning The Sky Fell Down In Florida 187

Attention! Laundry Room—333 Sunset Ave, Palm Beach, Fla..............189

Turn Left Or Turn Right 191

Time Spent Alone In Palm Beach, Fla 193

The Hamptons..195

Hearing..197

The House Guests 198

25 Things I Hate...199

Should We Eat Pizza Standing Up 201

My Son 204

I Know It's Not Important But It Keeps Eating At Me! 206

What I'm Looking Forward To 208

What To Do 210

August 23, 2011—My Earthquake.......................................211

My Hurricane...213

A Democratic Solution (Based On Lysistrata).......................215

Titles Of Former Books..216

ACKNOWLEDGMENT

Always to Elise Alarimo, where would I be without your major assistance. I positively cannot imagine how limited I would be.

Thank you XLibris for your usual help and dedication.

ADDENDUM

※

I've no time for writing
So don't even look
Because for the moment
This is my last book
(or maybe not . . . .)

GRANDMA HAS A TALE

This is not a bushy tail, or a long tail or even a fuzzy tail, but it is my *tale*. So here it is—my "Long Ago".

In my "long ago" there was no radio, TV, computers, IPads, air conditioning and many more no's.

There was just "after the first world war" and what came next, which happens to coincide with my childhood memories.

In this regard I will endeavor to recall as many incidents as I possibly can, and then perhaps my children, grandchildren and great grand kids will be able to envision me in a role other than Mom, gram, or big grandma.

Where to begin? That is indeed a problem. I think starting with my maternal grandparents would be best—so here goes.

My maternal grandparents arrived in America in either 1880 or 1881 and landed at Castle Gardens where the Battery Park Museum is now located—Ellis Island did not exist at that time.

They came from respectively—She Poland—He Germany (how they met I do not know). Both were 18 years old and were already married and accompanied by her brother and his mother.

I don't know whether my great grandmother (My grandfather's mother) came here with a husband, however I did ultimately learn that she had been married 4 times (no divorces) and died at the age of 95 falling down a flight of stairs enroute to a wedding (not hers). I can recall having met her once when I was about 7 and I believe we were much the same height. She was unbelievably tiny and wore a wig. We certainly had no particular relationship, but on the other hand I was very close to my mother's parents.

I believe they originally lived on the lower east side and had 11 children who all survived and flourished. My grandfather was in the men's clothing business and presumably was able to amply support his huge family.

My first recollection of them was when I was about 7 at which time they lived in Harlem on 111th Street in the upstairs of a 2 story brownstone.

I vividly recall having lunch there most Saturdays. We had to climb the outside stoop steps, where at the top there was a round white knob that when turned, it sounded a bell and the front door to the apartment then opened.

After that we had to climb several more steps to what appeared to be a long hall. To the left was the dining room with 2 angled windows in the front of which was a long leather sofa.

A large dining room table stood in front of that and to the complete left was an oak hutch with open shelves on top that housed various decorative dishes including a white porcelain cow that poured milk (I loved that little cow).

Straight ahead also on the left was the kitchen with a window on the right in front of which was a white marble topped table upon which my grandmother used to roll noodles for soup. Incidentally she called me "noodle poop" because I loved her soup (I still love soup). On the left side of the kitchen was the "ice box", and a wash tub. The black oven was on the right side.

Beyond that room was a small bedroom or sewing room where my youngest unmarried uncle slept and where grandma did her mending.

Getting back to the hallway—first came the bathroom which had a toilet with a ceiling high tank and a chain pull, then a sink and tub. Everything was painted apartment house tan.

From the hallway also to the right, the apartment became a railroad type. First came my youngest Aunt's bedroom with a white iron bed, a white armoire and a white dresser upon which she had a pin cushion with several black hat pins that I loved to touch.

Next came my grandparents bedroom with a large brass bed and another white armoire. I don't recall any chairs.

The living room came next which was furnished with a very attractive eggplant colored cut velvet sofa, 2 matching chairs with a Victorian white marble topped table between them.

An upright piano and my grandmother's rocker where on the extreme right. She always sat in that chair and reigned supreme when her family came to visit.

Two windows were straight ahead in between which was a long pier mirror with a marble shelf on the bottom.

By the way my grandmother's name was Ada (maiden name Brenner). I don't think she ever thought about diets as she was decidedly plump, with a round face, no wrinkles, huge beautiful brown eyes and very long white hair that she wore in what was known as a bun.

Her feet always seemed to hurt probably due to constantly standing while cooking and performing household duties.

These Saturday lunches at grandma's were always festive with many family members present. Aunts, uncles, cousins, plus various babies were usually visiting and had their particular places at the huge dining room table.

There were seltzer bottles at each end of the table and red wine as well, which was usually poured into the seltzer.

Chicken soup and all the familiar Jewish preparations were effortlessly served by grandma and for dessert we had the various cakes she had spent so much time baking.

I remember one time coming to visit her and passing a supposedly crippled man in the street lying on the sidewalk with a box in which he expected to receive monetary donations.

My mother who could never refuse to compensate a person in need gave him a generous sum. However on our return trip, we saw him glance furtively around and then get up and briskly walk away. So much for charity.

My grandfather was extremely handsome as were his four sons. Grandpa had a tiny moustache and wavy hair with a little curl on top—I used to love putting my index finger through that curl when I was little.

When grandpa arrived at Castle Gardens he was asked his name and answered Avram, which was Abraham in English. They repeated the question hoping to hear his last name—but again he answered Avram so the authorities named him Abraham Abrams. I don't think any of us ever knew his family name but he was always known as Mr. Abrams.

Incidentally he told me several times that he had been born during the civil war years—wow!!

GRANDMA ADA

I am very fortunate to remember my grandmother (my mother's mother) extremely well, and since we lived just a few blocks away during my youth, we visited on a regular basis.

My grandma was very Americanized as she and my grandfather arrived in America in 1880 and then proceeded to have 11 children.

My mother was the middle child and was born on July 5th. Grandma always referred to my mother's birthday as being "the day after the shooting". What she really meant was that it occurred the day after the July 4th fireworks.

At any rate, grandma Ada as everyone called her, spoke English very well, but still retained a slight foreign accent, which became very apparent after a particular incident.

My mother's youngest sister Martha was unmarried, and as was the custom in those days, she still lived at home with my grandparents.

One day a friend of Martha's called and asked to speak to her. Grandma politely asked who it was and the lady said Mrs. Abrams (grandma's last name) this is Yevette.

Grandma, not quite interpreting the name correctly, answered her in this manner. "Vell' I'm vashing but I'm not vet!

MEMORIES

While I attended Central Synagogue's services this past Yom Kippur, I found the sermon given by the Associate Rabbi, to be most intriguing.

She implied that at the end of our lives, the really special items left among our possessions were our memories, and she went on at length to explain how important these things can be.

Each person of course has a different set of memories, but what we all have in common is the fact that all memories are free, easily transportable, and they don't take up much space.

You don't have to store them in a closet or on a shelf, or in a drawer. You can obtain them at will, they can be accumulated over time, they can be savored whenever the urge to do so pops up, and all in all most memories can be the most treasured possessions of a person's life. They are also unique unto the individual.

Some memories can be distasteful, sad, or even horrible, but this type of memory does not have to be uppermost in the minds of most people. The wonderful thing about dark and unpleasant recollections is that they can generally be suppressed, and only thought about occasionally.

My memories, thank heavens, I can fortunately recall starting from my early childhood and are mostly pleasant for which I am truly grateful. Additionally in my particular case, I have lived long enough, and in so many places, that I have accrued an abundance of incidents from my lifetime that allow me to wander into my past for an extensive length of time, and thus "my tale" has evolved and resulted into the contents within these pages.

So whomsoever reads about my past experiences I do hope you enjoy doing so. I know I've loved living every moment of it.

WAY WAY BACK WHEN

The very first memory I have is a dream of a baby in a brass crib (me) crying, and experiencing the presence of a woman hovering over my crib and frightening me. At the time I remember thinking that this was not an actual person, but the bust of a marble statue that was on a pedestal in our living room.

I immediately awakened and realized that the woman was my mother who no doubt was standing there in response to my crying. I was probably no more than 3 years old as I was still in a crib.

Ever since, however I have disliked marble statuary, but of course I loved my mother.

My first home was 674 West 161st Street on Washington Heights in New York where I lived until the age of 6 ½. We lived on the second or third floor in the second apartment house next to Riverside Drive, which at that time had a split rail fence instead of the stone wall that now exists.

I distinctly recall 2 little friends from that early time—one of them, Pearl Osborne had an older brother who had what was known as a crystal set. This was the forerunner of a radio and when I visited Pearl, this unusual item always fascinated me.

The other friend was Lorraine Dickler whose apartment was opposite mine in the courtyard and we always conversed through our dining room windows. During one conversation she mentioned that she could only see out of one eye, which concept I could not quite understand. In fact when I actually saw her face to face I realized there was no pupil in that one eye.

Another early recollection at that address was of attending Miss Birdie and Miss Sidney's kindergarten class which existed on approximately 163rd or 164th Street on the corner of Riverside Drive—the bathroom stalls had no doors and I remember thinking that the toilets were very tiny and low. The school was opposite what we used to call the Deaf And Dumb Asylum where many unfortunate, hearing disabled children were forced to wear grey uniforms with Nehru collars and army type visor hats. To this day the memory of those little children profoundly disturbs me.

WAY BACK WHEN

I am pleased to say that I am one of those fortunate individuals who has almost total recall of early childhood events. However I beg you not to ask me what happened yesterday.

In any case I distinctly remember the entire layout of the 6 room apt I shared with my sister and parents when I was 4, including the colors and placement of the furnishings.

Floral printed cretonne slipcovers, with mothballs tucked into the corners, that covered the living room sofa and 2 chairs during the summer, are still vivid in my memory, down to the camphor odor.

Since we only lived in this apartment until I was 6 ½, this is really a long time recollection.

One incident I shall never forget is when I apparently had a severe ear infection, and our doctor (in those days he would come to the house for $5.00 a visit) tried to examine me in my bed but couldn't reach my head easily enough, and asked me to please turn upside down, thinking that I would place my head at the foot of the bed—instead I took him, literally and stood on my head!

As you can see—my childhood certainly had its ups and downs.

DEATH IN THE AFTERNOON

When I was about 4 years old I vividly remember being in a motion picture theatre in Asbury Park, New Jersey, during the summer.

When the film was over (it was the first one I'd ever seen), I emerged from the theater with my older sister. We immediately heard a tremendous amount of noise, there were many people loudly weeping and newsboys were hawking their papers that had enormous black headlines. There was general disorder prevailing and I finally learned the reason.

Rudolph Valentino had died! This was a major calamity in the motion picture world—but to me at 4 years old it didn't mean anything as I had never heard of him.

THE IMPORTANT LESSONS OF MY LIFE

Once upon a time there was a little girl—me—and I lived with my parents in New York City enjoying a very normal little girl existence. However during said childhood, the following events occurred, which shaped my philosophy of life forever. They also influenced my personality, judgment and behavior to this day.

My first recollection of these incidents was when I was very very young, during which time I spent the month of July with my parents at a hotel in Fleishman's NY followed by the month of August at a hotel in Asbury Park, NJ.

This arrangement took place every summer because air conditioning did not exist at that time and apartments in NY were unbearably hot during those 2 months.

At any rate when we were at the hotel in Fleischmans during my 5th year, I used to walk to the children's playground early every morning and along the way I passed an apple tree fully loaded with fruit and underneath which there was always a ripe apple on the ground. That apple was delicious and I thoroughly enjoyed it.

One day, as I was wholeheartedly munching my find, I met another child who asked me where I got it. I told her exactly under which tree I found my juicy treat and the next day when I followed my usual path there was no apple under the tree.

MORAL - KEEP YOUR MOUTH SHUT!

The next event also took place when I was 5 and, attended Miss Birdie and Miss Sidney's kindergarten class. During a show and tell event one morning, I proudly displayed an ivory open work fan my Aunt had brought me from Europe. Another child showed the class her 2 sided lollypop—red on one side and green on the other end. I salivated for it and at her suggestion we traded my fan for her lollypop. After I finished the pop, holding just the empty stick I realized she still owned the fan.

MORAL - DON'T BE GREEDY AND BEWARE OF BARGAINS!

Also when I was about 5 a little girl with whom I had been playing, said to me in a very snide manner, "my dress is prettier than yours". I knew that my dress was much prettier than hers so I vehemently told her so. There was a confrontation during which we both exchanged smacks. I hit her last and quickly ran home. Then, not bothering to wait for the elevator I ran up the staircase. But too late—she ran after me, yanking at and tearing my beautiful dress.

I fell down the stairs backwards, landing on my head and causing an egg sized bump which my mother fruitlessly tried to push down with a 50 cent piece; however I still have that bump.

MORAL - DON'T BE A BRAGGART AND NEVER ENGAGE IN PHYSICAL CONTACT

Then when I was 6 I had a nursemaid, Margaret whom I dearly loved. At any rate, one day, my little friend Pearl Osborne and I were strolling down the street and we suddenly came to the curb where in the gutter was a small change purse. Margaret said "Bernice pick it up". I foolishly replied "no it's dirty". However, my little friend Pearl voluntarily picked it up and found that it contained $7.00. Naturally she kept the money, and so I learned not to be so finicky about dirt, and also to pick up every penny I found in the street. To this day I've acquired a multitude of coins this way, but I doubt whether the accumulation has ever reached $7.00. C'èst La Vie!

MORAL - "FINDERS KEEPERS". DON'T BE FINICKY AND A LITTLE DIRT WON'T HURT!

At approximately age 8 I was with my little friend Edith Weisel and we started to argue about something nonsensical—I do not remember the reason—however in the midst of the argument Edith started to look like a monkey and it occurred to me that I probably looked like one too—at that moment I realized that arguing was foolish and that looking like a monkey was not pleasant—therefore I vowed never to *needlessly* argue again. I hope I've succeeded.

MORAL - KEEP YOUR COOL BESIDES NOBODY CAN ALWAYS BE RIGHT.

At last we come to age fifteen. I had finally met a "boy" and he wanted to kiss me. I said "no" and he wanted to know why not. I told him all my young girl friends and I had made a pact never to let a boy kiss us until age 18. He then told me that he had already kissed 4 of those girls!

MORAL - I THEREFORE DECIDED TO MAKE MY OWN DECISIONS FOREVER AND NOT TO BELIEVE EVERYTHING I WAS TOLD.

I must say these lessons have stood me in great stead all my life, sadly tho I'm not sure I've learned any other such major influences since those early experiences.

EMPLOYMENT ENJOYMENT?

My first job was at the age of 5 for which I was paid 5¢ a week to sweep the sidewalk on the corner of 161st and Audebon Avenue where some older children were in business on grocery crates, selling handmade doll clothes. I was supposed to keep their enterprise tidy and clean.

Because my job was considered to be a highly paid sinecure, there was no requirement for a union card, but I did have to bring my own broom.

One day I remember being a little weary after a particularly tedious sweeping time, and decided to rest in a friend's car at the curb.

Unfortunately, I slammed the car door on my index finger, and sat there screaming while my finger swelled and the blood coagulated.

Naturally because I was not union affiliated, I was unable to receive any disability funds—therefore I had to quit my job!

NEVER PIN YOUR HOPES TOO HIGH

One other incident in my life is still vivid in my memory—it was my 6th birthday and I was having a party in my home.

We were playing "pin the tail on the donkey" and wonder of wonders I won hands down. I didn't peek, I really put the tail right on target.

The prize was a little string of pearls which I coveted, except that I could not receive it—I couldn't buck the system. I was up against "the hostess rule". This rule is powerful and indefensible, you cannot receive a first prize if you are a hostess. It must be ceded to the next person in line—period!

Naturally there was only one thing I *could* do. I started to sob—I sobbed hysterically and then flung myself under my mother's bed where I thoroughly bemoaned this injustice regarding the pearls and remained until after the ice cream had been served.

Then of course it was time for me to blow out the candles on my cake, so I had to come out—"the hostess rule" did not apply in this instance, therefore I was the only 6 year old person at the party who could legally blow out the candles.

I also had another disappointment that day. I received many gifts but only one that was definitely *not* to my liking.

My cousin gave me a manicuring set complete with scissors, files, a nail buffer and several other small items which fit snuggly in a leather case. I hated it—it wasn't a toy—it was a real thing—for grown ups!

Besides, I was now 6 and perfectly able to bite my nails to a desired size. I certainly didn't need that case to help me.

Thank heavens I also received, a Parcheesi board and doll trunk among my other gifts, otherwise this birthday would have been a complete disaster! Moral—Don't be a sore loser—be a gracious hostess and good sport.

POTSY

Potsy, otherwise known as hopscotch played an important role in my life for various reasons.

1. I generally won because I had long legs and could usually avoid stepping on lines in the hopscotch grid.

2. It taught me to use discretion and great care as to where I would ever step.

3. Unfortunately it also made me become superstitious, as I was never able to put the keys (which we used to throw) into number *seven* and to this day I avoid anything with that number.

4. It was a wonderful friendship participation activity.

5. I'm so glad I still remember playing it.

6. But I'm sad that I'm still so superstitious about number *seven*.

A CRACK IN THE SIDEWALK

When I was very young—approximately 7 or 8, I would usually spend my Saturday afternoons with my father.

My mother and sister generally went shopping together, or to a Broadway show or movie.

Since my sister was 10 years older than I, these activities were deemed more suitable for her.

Around that time I was also informed that my mother had lost another child several years before, which accounted for the difference in ages between my sister and myself.

It was a long time before I realized that my mother had not misplaced that other child, but that she had unfortunately passed away.

At any rate I dearly loved my Saturday adventures with my father. We would do what I considered to be very exciting things.

Sometimes we would go to the aquarium on the lower east side, where I loved seeing varicolored sea creatures of many varieties. They were always just swimming around and seemingly looking straight at me with their mouths open. They could easily have been trying to talk.

Afterwards we would have lunch at the Automat on 34th Street which was the best treat of all.

The walls of the Automat were entirely filled with little drawers within which were many enticing types of food. In a way it was like the aquarium, except these drawers contained food, although fish might have been one of the varieties. For a number of nickels, which had to be popped into the drawer slots, out would come the best looking and best tasting items.

I loved the Automat, indeed it was my favorite Saturday place.

My skinny little frame which defined my body at the time was able to accommodate many kinds of food, and because I was allowed to insert the nickels, it was like going to Las Vegas, even though at the time I didn't know that place existed.

After lunch we would walk up Fifth Avenue and my father would make me an offer I couldn't refuse.

He said, if I didn't step on the cracks in the sidewalk, he would take me to FAO Schwartz to buy anything I desired. What an offer that was!

However if you have never tried to do this, especially at age 7 or 8, you would soon realize that this required dexterity beyond *my* tender years.

I would hobble along in my Mary Janes, one foot in front of the other, narrowly missing the cracks, and taking an interminable amount of time.

My father would take big steps, which meant I had to try keeping up with him, so getting to FAO Schwartz seemed almost impossible.

Nevertheless, eventually I sometimes succeeded in reaching that great store without stepping on a crack.

Then my life took on a magical twist! There is really nothing as fantastic as being an 8 year old let loose in FAO Schwartz.

No wonder I loved Saturdays with my dad.

ON WITH THE MEMORIES

These early recollections of my childhood do not compare with the more sophisticated events that occurred in the lives of my own children during their formative years. My memories are much sweeter and more innocent.

My children spent many of their young years in Florida, enjoying warm climate activities, whereas I grew up in a simpler time and in a cold winter environment. I had no electronic devices like the ones that exist today, nevertheless my memories are heartfelt and nostalgic.

One example at age 8 is still extremely vivid to me. We had already moved to 527 West 157th Street to a brand new apartment house on a hill, and as I recall, the winters back then seemed more severe, with heavy snow accumulating on the street making it possible to go sleigh riding down the hill. We used to call this belly whopping and it was great fun.

The street would be closed at night because the city did not require snow removal for several days, therefore children could enjoy outdoor winter activities to their hearts delight and until all hours of the evening.

Of course it was necessary to wear extremely warm clothing during these times, such as leggings, warm caps, scarfs, mittens and bulky jackets in order to avoid getting frost bitten—a common occurrence back then.

Another game we all enjoyed when snow was on the ground, took place when we built forts out of the snow on either side of the street and equipped these forts with a load of snowballs.

This form of ammunition would be flung with great force onto the so called enemies on the opposite side.

Thankfully after a few cold hours of playing war, a thoughtful mother would invite the entire group into her apartment for hot chocolate and homemade cookies.

Nothing ever tasted so good! And the memory lingers on.

SUMMER CAMP

I was 9 years old and off to camp for the 1st time. It was supposed to be a wonderful experience for me, although I didn't realize my parents were probably very happy not to be responsible for me during the summer.

I went to camp Echo Lake in Readfield Maine, and in those years, it required an overnight train trip and then a rickety bus ride over bumpy unpaved roads to get to the camp site.

My bunk was for the youngest children at that time and housed 8 girls and one counselor, Pete (I think she was gay). It was also at the waters edge so the view was great.

I particularly remember not liking to make my bed, and decided that if I slept very quietly, I would be able to slip out from the top in the morning and then just smooth the blanket over the sheets, thus avoiding actual bed making. Being skinny at the time made this procedure very simple.

Today of course this system would not be possible as my present bathroom scale shows that I weigh on a heavier side so I am no longer able to slip out of my bed as I did in those early days.

Thinking back, I truly loved that first summer. It was wonderful being with such a great group of girls who were such fun, wonderful athletes and in many instances they became my lifelong friends.

Many years later 2 of my grandchildren went to the same camp, although the name had been changed to Camp Vega and they travelled there by airplane.

I was then fortunate enough to attend parents visiting day, (no parents or relatives were permitted in my day), and I actually saw my old bunk plus a few of the other original buildings that still existed.

Now my great granddaughter is there for the first time at age 8, but great grandparents are not on the present visiting list. At least I still have my memories.

HOW TO GET A JOB

When I was a young girl I was very much interested in learning details about my mother's early years.

I often begged her to relate anecdotes she thought I would enjoy hearing.

In this regard she told me the following:

She had graduated from Wadleigh High School in New York, and had attended Secretarial School in order to learn future job skills. In those days college education was a rarity.

At any rate my mother had a job interview with the William Morris theatrical agency and was asked to take some sample dictation.

The letter that was dictated to her involved the future employment requirements of some chorus girls, who apparently would have to wear tights during their performances while on the road.

My mother duly typed the letter and gave it to her would be employer. He read it and then asked if she would mind reading it out loud.

She started reading and when she got to the word "tights" she realized she had written "tits" and being embarrassed, she stopped reading.

The agency gentleman then laughed and said never mind reading anymore Miss Abrams—you're hired!

DON'T BE FOOLED BY GLITTER

At the time of my birth, my father who was a successful Jeweler at the time, asked my mother if she wanted him to give her a diamond pin or a baby grand victrola.

Being Jewish, my mother said "I'd like the diamond pin". A week later the victrola arrived in our apartment.

When my mother questioned this gift, my father said he thought she'd prefer it, because it was so unusual.

Shortly afterwards she got the diamond pin anyway, which was also very unusual. He actually made a replica of the Liberty Bell. The clapper was a large diamond that moved back and forth, there was also a large diamond in the middle, and where the crack appeared in the Liberty Bell, he made the crack of emeralds in the pin. Since my father made the pin himself, it became a family heirloom, which I inherited and then passed on to my granddaughter to ultimately bequeath to her daughter and so on.

However the "victrola" is another story. When I was small I loved sitting under it and used to sing along with all of Caruso's arias. My family owned most of his red seal recordings and because the victrola's top opened up just like in a grand piano, all I had to do was pop a record on the inside and sing to my heart's content.

Several years later my family purchased a baby grand piano and so the baby grand victrola was no longer appropriate to be in the same room as the new piano. 2 baby grands in the same area would be ridiculous—Where the victrola subsequently went?—I have no idea!

Nevertheless, at an antique show in the 1980's there was a man who had a vintage victrola exhibit. Being curious I asked him, if he ever came across a baby grand victrola. He said only a very few were ever made, and if one were ever discovered it would probably cost around $350 thousand dollars. The diamond pin never achieved that monetary status.

In retrospect my mother would have been better off being gentile!

"MOVING DAY" IN THE RENTAL ERA

Many years ago in New York City, October first was considered to be "Moving Day" and throughout the boroughs, truck company employees spent the entire day loading their vans with furniture from various rental apartments, to be delivered to the new residences people had leased.

On this day traffic was noticeably heavy, and the crowded car, bus and truck lanes led to furniture delivery delays, as well as frazzled nerves and short tempers.

In many instances children were sent to the homes of friends or relatives who were not moving, so that they would not get under foot nor bother their parents, or the movers during these busy times.

Luncheonettes and neighborhood delicatessens were busily preparing sandwiches, light lunches and dinners for irate husbands who were annoyed at being inconvenienced by having their households uprooted.

Wives however were extremely pleased to be moving, as it avoided having to live in their old apartments during an extensive paint job. Besides most landlords offered one or two months rent concessions on the newly rented apartments, which was a great incentive for frequent moving.

On the flipside, there were many occasions when heavy downpours occurred and much havoc ensued. Furniture got wet, floors were muddied, walls got dirtied, deliveries were mishandled and sent to some other person's apartment by mistake. Also prized possessions were either lost or broken, which was a real disaster. The worst situation was when furniture designated for a particular area did not fit when placed against the walls in the new apartment.

So instead of the prospect of happy new living conditions amid the Beauty of Autumn's "Bright Blue Weather," victims of October First's "Moving Day" often came to the conclusion that it was really a huge mistake.

Thus by the end of World War II, co-op apartments came into vogue, landlords mostly relied upon their commercial real estate holdings for income and "Moving Day" became a thing of the past.

THE WOMAN IN 8B

Almost everyone who was a resident of Manhattan in the years leading up to World War II is fairly familiar with the apartment situation that existed at the time—I'm referring to the 2 months rental concession that was part of most leases.

In those days, there were very few co-ops. People either lived in a private home in Brooklyn, Westchester or Long Island, or were compelled to rent an apartment in the Big City and were able to take advantage of the concession arrangement.

My family lived in an apartment in the upper west side of Manhattan and generally moved every 2 years because of the concession benefits, as well as not having to live with a paint job.

Our neighbors were usually lovely people, artistic, theatrically talented, some with cute little dogs, some with nice children, and even some who shacked up.

Unfortunately, occasionally there were those who noisily banged a lot on their pianos and kiddies who played bouncey ball overhead.

The most memorable one however, was the lady in 8B—just down the hall from our apartment. She cooked—boy did she cook! Usually smelly soup—smellier fish and a disgusting concoction of unknown varieties. It was quite unbearable for the two years we lived there.

But thanks to the concession arrangement we moved to another building to the top floor, on Riverside Drive where our only neighbor was the man who wrote "Mairzy dotes and Dozy dotes". He delighted us with his many tunes and the only thing we smelled was fresh air.

DEPRESSING TIMES

Several years ago Queen Elizabeth of England proclaimed a very sad time in her country, to be an "Annis Horribilus"

However in America the year 1929 definitely epitomized an equally dire situation. It was the year of the Wall Street crash that stunned so many people, ruined lives, caused a multitude of suicides, and was responsible for a number of lifestyle changes in most families.

So many of my friends had to move to other cities, neighborhoods and homes. There were apple vendors on every street corner in my area, and the prices of all consumer goods plummeted but were still not within reach of most people's purchasing power.

The luxuries in my life that I had always taken for granted were suddenly no longer affordable, and everyone I knew had to come to grips with our country's economic changes.

The word "depression" was on everyone's lips. President Hoover who was still in office was deemed to be a failure and everyAmerican was looking forward to a new regime and better times.

Europe was also in the midst of economic difficulties and Adolph Hitler's rise to power started to emerge.

The year 1932 brought President Franklin D. Roosevelt upon the scene, prohibition ended, and there was suddenly a little more hope in the air. He starting making his Sunday night fireside chats on the radio, and most families who had radios would gather around their sets and listen avidly to his every encouraging word.

But these were really tough times in our country although somehow people were more compassionate than they are today, and neighbors and friends tried to help each other.

Today there is a lack of community spirit, politicians are at each others throats and our futures do not seem as bright as they were envisioned to be during those depression times.

Nevertheless, we have always rallied from a multitude of drastic years in the history of America. So we have to hope that we will soon recover from our present frailty and once again become a country of accomplishment and world respect.

A REALLY SAFE PLACE

I distinctly recall a time of my youth when I lived on the upper west side of Manhattan in a very nice apartment house.

In those days only a few people I knew had private homes, unless they lived in the Bronx, Brooklyn, Westchester or New Jersey.

Apartment living in that period was mostly quite delightful. A doorman would greet you, carry your heavy packages, hail a taxi if necessary, and in general would make you feel safe when entering your building.

Elevator men would take you to your floor and wait until you opened your apartment door before descending downstairs.

It was a most gracious way to live. However on occasion, apartments had their downside.

A particular evening comes to mind. My parents were having a dinner party after which the entire group of guests retired to the living room in which we had a baby grand piano.

Actually no one played that piano but on that night it certainly proved to be useful.

You see New York apartments had many inhabitants other than the rent paying ones. I am referring to the infestation of ants, cockroaches and mice.

On that special evening a lively little mouse made his presence known, and before you could say Jack Robinson, 3 people were standing on our piano, in total confusion and dismay.

There was much shrieking and the rest of the guests scurried to different rooms in our apartment.

My mother, being the Hostess, jumped out of her chair and speedily ran into the kitchen, never to be seen again.

The mouse, I believe found another spot probably in a closet, and was also deemed to be gone forever.

Finally the people on the piano came down and returned to their various homes where hopefully no mice were present.

I doubt if they were ever able to either thank my mother for dinner or to bid her farewell. As I previously mentioned she did not emerge from the kitchen for several hours.

My father therefore had to assume the role of a fearless host.

I TRIED TO LAUGH BUT IT JUST WASN'T FUNNY

I think I was about 12 years old and was walking home from grade school, when I felt a sudden snap in my underwear.

In those years there existed something called a garter belt that attached to long stockings, which I happened to be wearing.

Unfortunately mine disengaged itself from my stockings and drooped down to the ground on 86th Street and Broadway in New York City. This happened on a Friday about 3:30 PM when loads of Jewish ladies were just emerging from Tip Toe Inn with their Friday night loaves of Chollah bread.

So there I was walking along carrying my books with two straggly garters hanging down between my legs and dragging on the ground.

I could feel all those Jewish eyes fixed on this strange and embarrassing sight, and didn't quite know what to do, so I tried to laugh and mumbled "hee hee hee I think I'm losing something", but it just wasn't funny.

MY MOTHER'S POSSIBLE ADVICE TO MY 18 YEAR OLD SELF

Dear Bernice,

You might as well know now that you will never amount to anything unless you learn the certain basics of how to succeed in life.

First of all, it is really essential to be able to boil water, an egg, or even a potato.

Secondly beds are meant to be made rather than just slept in.

Thirdly—remember to always have a handkerchief in your hand bag. Don't forget we have not yet invented Kleenex.

It would be nice too if you would offer to clear the table once on a while.

However if you can't master these minor accomplishments, perhaps it would be wise to marry a rich man so you wouldn't have to do any of the above.

Love—Mom

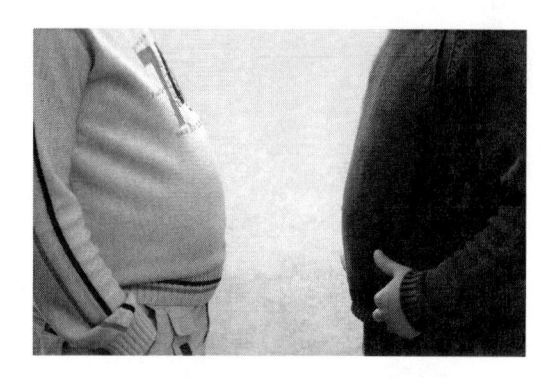

AS I RECALL, HE WAS CHUBBY, ETC

When I was about 19 everyone I knew was becoming engaged or getting married. The romances in my neighborhood (the 70's to 90's on the West Side of NY) abounded with showers, parties and notices in the Times.

It was an exciting time, nobody could figure out who would be next to announce some future nuptial. Would the "He" she selected be smart, handsome, tall, rich, funny, talented or whatever? We were all very anxious to hear the romantic details.

One Sunday afternoon during this decade an engagement party was being held at a good friend's home. She was a very beautiful girl and we couldn't wait to meet her handsome fiancé.

At the apartment door her mother greeted a group of us with these words—"it should happen to you".

We all walked into the living room where many people had gathered and in a corner was our friend with her fiancé. As I recall he was chubby, short, bald and wore thick glasses. I learned later that he was quite well to do.

However all I could think of at the time was—"please god don't let it happen to me".

HOW I GOT ENGAGED

Starting with the 1920's, the Sunday NY Times proudly published announcements of newly engaged couples, just as they did with marriages, deaths and newborns.

These columns were perused avidly by East and West siders alike, as usually 1 or 2 familiar names were listed.

Indeed, I too was a peruser, and I had hoped that one day my name along with that of a handsome young swain would be on that page.

Sure enough the day finally arrived in 1941 when I was a listee, but the events leading up to it were rather unusual.

For instance, I met my future husband in Peoria Illinois and our courtship was mostly via telephone calls, postage stamp interchange and visiting back and forth until we both realized an engagement was in the offing.

At that time Al (my husband to be) wanted to present me with a ring and since my father was a jeweler, it was obvious that the ring should be purchased from him, especially at the wholesale price.

Naturally I had to ask Al via telephone how much he wanted to spend, which was rather awkward, and it was even worse when I personally had to pick out the ring myself.

My mother and I then made arrangements to go to Illinois to bring the ring to Al so he could give it to me. At that time my engagement became somewhat of a negotiable proceeding particularly when my father said I had to ask Al for the money before I gave him the ring.

When I arrived in Peoria with the ring box in tow, I picked a propitious time to give Al the ring, so he in turn could present it to me.

The absolutely most terrible moment came when I had to tell him my father said I had to be sure to get the money first before the ring changed hands. (Thank God I got Al's check).

As you can see, my engagement was a complete business transaction and totally unlike what I was hoping for it to be.

It wasn't until I actually read my announcement in the NY Times that the romantic aspect of this event actually kicked in.

ANTI SEMITISM

I first experienced anti semitism when I got married and moved to Peoria, Illinois. Before that, and during most of my growing up years on the upper West Side of New York all my neighborhood friends were Jewish and practically all of my school mates as well. But since my parents were not members of a temple, I had very little knowledge of my Jewish roots. In fact, I had never even heard of Hanukah and none of my friends' brothers had ever been Bar Mitzvahed. Thus when I moved to Peoria where there were only 225 Jewish families and out of necessity all of them were ardent temple attendees, I soon found myself realizing that being Jewish was not acceptable in Peoria and apparently a no no in most of Middle America.

One day as I was riding the bus to the downtown section of Peoria (I did not drive in those years), the lady next to me with whom I had been chatting in a neighborly fashion, suddenly said "do you see that woman getting on the bus? She's Jewish and you know the Jews have all the money". I remember cringing and being afraid to admit that I too was "one of those". (I also wondered where all that money was!).

A year or so later I was on a train enroute to Fort Worth Texas where I was going to meet Al, as the 2nd World War had broken out and that city was going to be our home for the next unknown period of time.

My fellow passenger was a priest and we pleasantly passed the time in a conversational manner. At one point he asked me what church I attended and I replied, "I am Jewish and go to a temple". He thought for a long moment and then said "you know I have some Indian blood". I'm sure he presumed that we were therefore on a somewhat equal basis.

Fort Worth in those war years was overly populated with soldiers and other people from all over the United States who were working for Consolidated Vultee, which was one of the leading manufacturers of airplanes in the U.S. and where Al was also employed.

However this influx of people caused a shortage of housing. We had contacted the Chamber of Commerce and were given a few telephone numbers for apartment availabilities, and were continually disheartened when they came to no avail. Finally a Mrs. Margaret Levy (not Jewish) told us she had a lovely empty apartment and assured us that we would like it.

However when I told her my name she asked "are you Jewish". Of course I said yes and was then told that the apartment was in a Baptist community and she didn't think we'd be happy there.

We were finally able to share an adorable little house with one of Al's co-workers and lived there all during the war years. Luckily the owner moved to California after 6 months so we were then able to have the house to ourselves.

Incidentally when Al first worked at Consolidated he was asked where were his "horns" as they heard that all Jewish men had "horns". They finally accepted him as one of their own because he beat them at horseshoe pitching.

At this point I must say that the most wonderful friends we ever had and whom we could count on in stressful times were our non Jewish friends. Sarah June and Philip Goode and Jack and Flora Winnick from Ft. Worth, and Juliet and Jerry Connolly from Palm Beach can never be forgotten for the outstanding things they did for us and for the truly amazing friendships we all shared. However, the many many great Jewish friends we've had and still have made us realize how fortunate we have been throughout the years, regardless of religion.

FOUR LETTER WORDS

Starting in my early childhood I was informed by my parents and teachers ---- using ---- letter words was absolutely verboten.

I tried to avoid their usage, and believe my successful marks regarding the avoidance of these words was 100%.

Nevertheless "abstaining" became extremely difficult.

Why was it difficult? Because after finally meeting a particularly great person and hoping to marry him, I was unable to say the words "I ---- you".

However we ultimately did get married and after a period of a few years, I wanted to announce my pregnancy to him. I was actually having a ----! But could indicate it simply my poking my stomach.

Yes I had the ---- and she was beautiful and healthy. She arrived in Texas, where we lived, but shortly afterwards we intended moving to New ----.

I could not reveal my moving whereabouts to my parents and friends because of my inability to use any ---- letter information.

Finally, though, I got rid of my inhibition, moved to New *York* and now I *even* have hot *soup* on a *cold* day!

P.S. Also you'd be surprised by some of my current vocabulary.

MY FATHER'S FAMILY

My father's family were totally different from my mother's family—My mother's relatives each had a very good sense of humor, were fun loving, very family oriented and always shared a close association with each other.

In direct contrast my father's family considered themselves to be intellectuals, and for the most part were socialistically inclined and agnostic, although they did enjoy traditional Jewish food. They had very few family associations, consequently I had almost no contact with any of them as a young child. I never met my grandmother and only met my grandfather once.

From what I understand my great grandfather had some kind of business establishment in Russia that the then Czar patronized, and therefore he was granted a "privilege" which enabled his children to attend school and live in Moscow. Maybe this was why the following generations became such snobs.

At any rate when the new Czar came into power he apparently hated the Jewish people and thus my grandparents had to hastily leave Russia. They came to America in the year 1883 with 2 children who had been born in Moscow, and they had 7 others in America.

Many of my father's family members were quite creative and artistically inclined. One cousin of mine was an outstanding lace designer. She later married the President of the Macy Store in Toledo, and one of her sons married a well known fine art restorer. Two of my other cousins were professional artists, 2 were interior designers (I was also) and still another cousin married a successful author. One of his books became the film "Letter To 3 Wives". Their son I was led to believe, invented the slogan "Where's The Beef". In addition, a cousin of my grandfather was a renowned poet in Russia and I think there is a street named after him in Tel Aviv.

My father and one of his brothers were very talented Jewelry designers and artisans. They made beautiful jewelry consisting mostly of diamonds and precious colored stones. Then in the year 1905 at the age of 21 my father went into the jewelry business for himself and was extremely successful until his death in 1953.

Sometime in the 1920's he opened a beautiful shop on Broadway and 47th Street with a uniformed doorman to guard the premises, and established a large theatrical clientele.

What with the Palace Vaudeville Theater, and all the Broadway shows that were in the area, his friendship with many producers and well known theatrical performers enabled him to acquire house seats for most opening night productions, plus being able to sell many celebrities his lovely jewelry.

As a result, I went to the Palace Theater every Friday night to see these world famous vaudeville performers, and I also attended most Broadway shows with my parents, starting at age 6. I met so many famous theatrical people that I simply took it for granted, and considered it to be the average situation in every child's life.

But in depression years my father's business declined. Many of his loyal customers committed suicide owing him a great deal of money, and most people could no longer afford expensive jewels, so there were a few years of non luxurious living for our family.

However in 1940 things changed. In addition to his regular business on 5th Avenue and 48th Street, my father opened several jewelry shops in the Seiden family Resort Hotels—The Laurel-In-The-Pines in Lakewood, New Jersey, The Grand Hotel in High Mount, New York and the Lido Hotel in Lido Beach, Long Island.

All of a sudden a lot of people started making money again. The European war made the manufacturing of army items a very big deal in New York, war contracts abounded and expensive jewelry once again was much in demand.

After the usual type of upper west side girlhood that I experienced, walking on Broadway most Sunday afternoon between 72nd and 96th Streets, attending temple junior league groups in order to meet boys, going to parties, dating various young men, plus a few special romances and in general having a happy time, I met my future husband Al Zakin while visiting a cousin in Peoria, Illinois.

Peoria, Illinois

I must say this was a very exciting trip. I had never been out of the New York area, other than for my camp years in Maine. However this time I was on my own and when I arrived in Peoria my cousin arranged to have the local newspaper photographer come by to take my picture (which I still have). It was a full page and announced that a visiting cousin from New York had come to this little town. Very exciting local news indeed! (In New York nobody could have cared less that I was there).

Everybody entertained me as was the local custom—they had luncheons and dinners and I was obligated to accept dates. When I told my cousin I didn't think it appropriate for me to have any local young men spend money on a temporary visitor, she said that if I didn't accept these invitations people would think there was something wrong with me. So I dated.

At a luncheon one day a girl asked me who my date was for Saturday night. I told her it was someone named Zokin or Zakin—She then said "you'll like him, he's sophisticated". I thought to myself "humph—Peoria sophistication". However she was right—Al was different from my other dates in Peoria as well as the young men I dated in New York, and we got along swimmingly. In fact we had a few dates and when I got to the train station for my trip back home, he arrived with a jar of sour balls, which I had mentioned on one of our dates, that I liked very much. It was a nice gesture so I gave him a 2¢ stamp and told him to write me a letter.

Thus began a correspondence friendship and after many telephone calls and back and forth visits to and from Peoria and New York we decided to save postage stamps and stationary and get married. So you see our marriage was based on economy and thrift!

In June 1941, and after our honeymoon in Williamsburg, Virginia, we finally arrived in Peoria and were able to rent a lovely apartment in a 2 family house for $67.50 a month and proceeded to settle down as newlyweds.

I must say I thoroughly loved living there. Everyone was so warm and welcoming. Al had many friends and they all accepted me as one of their own. Most New Yorkers have a very poor reputation in the Midwest due to their attitudes of superiority when meeting Midwesterners. Knowing this I quickly learned to never verbally compare New York customs to those of the Midwest, and indeed I came to realize that the Midwesterners are warm, hospitable, charitable, bright and just as worldly as most New York people believe *they* are.

Peoria is also where I learned to cook and bake—abilities at which all the young Jewish wives were extremely adept. In New York no young married girls cooked. They ordered in—ate at their parents homes, or ate out, and some had live in help who cooked.

Peoria had no such thing as caterers and no place from where it was possible to order in and since my parents lived far away, I had to learn the art of cookery. So after spending 6 months practicing my culinary efforts I was finally able to compete favorably with my new friends and prepared an all home cooked dinner party which was successful—my mother, who was an excellent cook and baker even though we had full time help, sent me innumerable recipes which included drawings indicating directions as to how to place a roast beef in a pan etc. (I still have those letters).

Sports were very important in this town and since my husband was a very low handicap golfer, I had to learn how to play. However this did not come easily as I was a constant whiffer. Al (and I believed him) had an explanation for this situation. He said that the ground in Peoria was 2 inches lower than New York and consequently I was unable to hit the ball in Peoria. A "ball" faced lie!

There were also only 225 Jewish families living in Peoria but it included many famous ones.

As for instance Ben Frankel who founded the first Hillel Society in America, which ultimately appeared on most college campuses and still does. His daughter Ernestine Walk became my very good friend.

Then there was Sam Rothberg and Julian Venezky (he was the best man at our wedding). They both were internationally renowned as the founders of the American Friends of the Hebrew University and were instrumental in the founding of the U.J.A. They both had great ties to

Israel and a very personal relationship with Golda Meir. Recently they have both passed away.

Ellie Goodman, who is still my very good friend, was the mother of Susan G. Komen who passed away from breast cancer many years ago, and is remembered internationally by the organization in her name, and founded by her sister Nancy Brinker, who lives in Palm Beach, and was the American Ambassador to Hungary during the Bush administration.

Another one of my Peorian friends, Ann Gordon was once married to a "Dead End Kid" of the motion pictures.

Betty Friedan was also a Peorian, although I did not know her. Her parents had a small jewelry shop in town, but there was no indication then of her future fame.

There were also many other influential residents in this little town, whose names escape me at present.

Because in the Midwest there is a thing called Jewish geography, everyone Jewish all over the country somehow has a connection with each other. Therefore wherever you go you are bound to know someone who knows someone else you know. This makes it very easy to make friends all over the country.

Belatedly, I have to say that my life in Peoria made me aware of being not *only Jewish*, but a *"Jew"*. This was because I had grown up on the West Side of Manhattan as a Marjorie Morningstar kind of person and was not at all observant.

However in Peoria where the Jewish people were such a minority, they had to make their presence known for good deeds and philanthropic endeavors—and they certainly did!

Consequently it was essential that the entire Jewish community participate in all temple affairs and charitable organizations—thus I became a member of a temple for the first time.

But what I found to be extremely fortunate when I lived there were the wonderful friendships I developed and still maintain, and to become an enthusiastic citizen of this most unique small town.

Sadly on December 7th, 1941 World War II broke out in America and since Al had a very low number in the selective service system, he attempted to apply for a commission in the army, and arranged for an appointment in Chicago in order to do so. However on the day before the appointment he played football and injured his knee, so when he limped into the army office, they put him into 4F but made it mandatory that he remain in the service and he was then sent to New York to become a purchasing agent for war materiel on the eastern coast.

This meant that we would have to uproot, put our newly purchased furniture in storage and leave Peoria where we had been so happy. Subsequently we moved to New York City.

We rented an apartment in a hotel opposite my parent's apartment, which made it very convenient for visiting and having free dinners with them on a regular basis. A very smart decision.

Also my sister who was the head of the talent department at Warner Brothers Pictures New York office, was able to get a job there for me.

My job was not time consuming nor important, and happily I became fast friends with the girl who sat next to me as well as the girl behind me. The girl in front of me was Lauren Bacall's cousin. Nobody had much work to do, so at 10:30 every morning all of us went to the ladies room to play gin rummy. At 12 we all went to lunch, and at 2:30

we went back to the ladies room to continue our game. Thank heavens no one ever discovered our work habits.

It's a really good thing however, that Warner Brothers had many other more loyal employees.

By the way, the girl who sat beside me at Warner's was very beautiful and her brother in law was the head of all the New York Warner theaters, so when she met and then married "Moe" of the "Three Stooges" on the stage of the Strand Theater, we all attended the wedding and then they both moved to California.

After several months she found out that Moe had severe mental problems due to being hit in the head so often during his role on the "Three Stooges" and they were divorced.

Subsequently we introduced her to one of Al's friends in Peoria and they got married and moved there. Of course I was the Matron of Honor. The man who performed the service was Rabbi Segal whose son was Erich Segal who wrote the book and movie "Love Story". This Rabbi always ended his marriage services with the phrase "Legal By Segal" and was very popular because of his humor.

FORT WORTH, TEXAS ALSO KNOWN AS COW TOWN

When my husband Al and I lived in Forth Worth, Texas during part of World War II, it was one of the most exciting experiences of our lives.

We were lucky enough to become friends with many wonderful people from every state in the union, as well as native Texans.

Our immediate neighbors next door were the Unger Bungers (as we called them) from the Midwest, the Truex's on the other side of us were from Rochester, New York. Mez Truex was so tidy that she would not allow anyone to enter her house without first removing their shoes. She had a 2 year old son, and instead of cuddling a dirty blanket as most little ones do, this baby carried a clean diaper everyday. Also Mez's bathroom floor tiles had snow white grouting. It was never stepped on with anything other than bare feet.

Across our sizeable yard were our best friends, the Goodes. They were from College Station, Texas and I spent most of my free time with Sarah June Goode who was extremely bright and very funny and I truly loved being with her.

Across the street were the Bermis from Pittsburgh. She was trying desperately to become pregnant and was quite jealous when I announced that I was expecting a baby. In fact on the few occasions that we were in their car, (we had none at the time) her husband would deliberately go over bumps in the road with great force presumably hoping that I would miscarry. They were not our favorite people.

Another neighbor across the street sat on her porch everyday counting pennies into a bucket and when the coins reached a certain amount they went into a huge carton (the pennies not the neighbors). These people owned gum ball machines and this was how they prepared their earnings to deposit into the bank.

Seymour and Yetta Farber were also from Pittsburgh and just about 8 years ago we were pleasantly surprised to have them call us. I imagine at least 50 years had transpired since we saw them. They were coming to New York for a wedding and decided to call to see if we were still alive—they actually came to visit us and we were so happy to have that reunion. You never know when your past will catch up with you.

Most of our neighbors had wartime jobs as did Al, at the Consolidated Vultee Airplane Factory. However we also knew full time local Texans who became good friends—the Cohen's, the Winnicks, and the Wolfs.

Florence Cohen was a fabulous cook, as are most Midwesterners and Southerners, and I still have all the wonderful recipes she gave me. They were also responsible for introducing us to all the local Jewish people.

Toby and Ann Wolf were originally from New Orleans but had presumably settled in Fort Worth before World War II. Toby was in the jewelry business in Fort Worth but his army commitment compelled him to work at Consolidated during the war, so he and Al were together a great deal.

The Winnicks were very special people in our lives. They were originally from Peoria where Jack had been a very good friend of one of Al's brothers.

He and Al met in the local golf locker room and Al recognized Jack's accent and voice as being from Peoria—Subsequently we became very good friends. Jack owned the shoe department in one of the large department stores in Fort Worth and his entire family adopted us. Flora Winnick was Catholic, Jack was Jewish, their daughter Joanie was Episcopalian and their daughter Barbara was a Methodist. Their 2 year old son had no religious affiliation. However this family honored each member's religion and always attended each of their individual church and religious holidays together, a truly wonderful arrangement.

Joanie Winnick age 14 kindly drove me to my obstetrician every week, (we had no car and besides I did not know how to drive) and we also had dinner with them at their home every Sunday. Nobody could have been more kind to perfect strangers from the east. The Winnicks were truly unique and the memory of their friendship will never be forgotten.

Forth Worth people in those days were extremely involved in local politics and had an intense loyalty to Texas. For instance, when we went to the movies, the locals always stood and sang "The Eyes of Texas Are upon You" before the picture started.

Also very few people ever wore shoes in the buses, and I was never sure when or if we were going to secede from the United States. It was a constant threat that secession was about to take place. In fact I remember calling my mother and saying "don't worry if you don't hear from me, I think we are going to secede. Thank heavens this never took place.

Another unusual Texan tradition at that time was that if you went to a store to make a purchase, you might be forced to wait forever for a salesperson to wait on you—however when you finally were able to complete a purchase that same salesperson would say "hurry back now you'all". Quite a dichotomy. In addition, if you ask for directions to a place, they would be apt to say "it's just down the road a piece"

We like all the other temporary inhabitants had a great deal of trouble finding a suitable place to live when we first arrived in Fort Worth, as good housing there was a major problem. We had contacted the Chamber of Commerce on several occasions and read the ads in the local paper as well, but there we were, still holed up in the Hotel Jefferson.

Finally though we hit the jackpot. Al met a girl at work who was willing to have us share her brand new house which was really adorable. It was on one acre and had 2 bedrooms one of which would be ours, plus a kitchen (we'd share) and a sizeable living room, dining room combination (we'd also share).

There was practically no furniture in the living room, dining room combination, just a very stiff sofa and four small dining chairs and a table. There was also a non working fireplace—it was supposedly a decorative item. All in all it became our little paradise especially when our land lady, Janetta Deigh decided to move to California and we were able to rent the entire house—Happy Day!

When our baby Nancy was born she inherited the second bedroom which was commodious and had its own bathroom—At last we were a family!

As a bonus we were able to acquire the weekly services of a lovely housekeeper—Viola—who lived in a trolley car and kindly gave us many of her unneeded food stamps. This was a real blessing as we had to do a lot of home cooking.

Viola was the mainstay of our lives at the time, and 40 years later when she was visiting in New York, she called us. How she found our telephone number I can't imagine. At any rate we found out that she'd become the head of the entire nursing staff at the hospital in Texas where Nancy was born. This was indeed a very great honor for her. Since she was leaving the next day we could not get together, however when she got home she sent us her picture. She had become a beautiful white haired lady and the photo is still a treasured keepsake.

Our Texas days were wonderful despite the wartime situation. We will always be grateful for the graciousness with which we were accepted into such a terrific community.

WELCOME TO THE WORLD

During World War II Al and I lived in Fort Worth, Texas, where the army appointed him as the Head of the Treasury Department of Consolidated Vultee (the leading airplane manufacturer at that time), and he in turn tried to convert me into a "sort of" competent cook and housewife. As we soon learned, I also had to acquire future mothering abilities and skills.

Luckily we had wonderful neighbors, developed great friendships, and everyone was most solicitous of my advancing condition, and they were also aware of my complete ignorance about infants.

Since we had no car, a particular couple, (the Winicks) arranged to have me delivered in their vehicle, to all my medical appointments.

The car was usually driven by their 14 year old daughter. Her very young age driving license was sanctioned by the Ft. Worth Department of Vehicles and was perfectly legal, according to Texas authorities. Naturally, it was completely unnerving to my New York background.

However we never had any unfortunate driving incidents during these medical visits, and thereafter starting pre-naming the baby "Julius", as we considered that to be a fairly unattractive name and pessimistically figured that it (the baby) would be both homely and a boy.

Eventually "Julius" decided to arrive and my husband heroically intended driving me to the hospital in our own 2 seater car which we had acquired a few days previously.

By this time my mother had arrived from New York to welcome her first grandchild.

Unfortunately when all 3 of us (almost 4) squashed into the two seater, we discovered that there was NO gas, so again we had to call upon other friendly neighbors (the Goodes) to get us to the hospital to meet "Julius".

In those days they put expectant mothers out completely, therefore it wasn't until I woke up in the recovery room that I realized I was a mother and asked the nurse in attendance "how is *he*". She replied *She* is wonderful" which was not the answer I expected.

Nevertheless my husband and I were extremely thrilled, especially when we first laid eyes upon our very beautiful little girl Nancy.

Since it was wartime, the hospital was understaffed and overfilled, consequently Nancy's first accommodations in the hospital was a dresser drawer.

I don't know whether it was French provincial, Victorian or maybe art deco, I only knew that it was small and she, being over 8 pounds, completely filled it.

Thank heavens when we arrived back in our little Texas house she had a real crib in which to sleep.

I must say that Nancy's future sleeping arrangements, all through these many years, have been most attractive and commodious.

So you never know what the future holds.

THOSE TEXAN YEARS

When my husband and I lived in Ft. Worth, Texas many years ago we went to a restaurant for lunch and he noticed an intriguing item listed on the menu, it was a "Yard Egg Omelet"—He was curious as to the contents of this item and asked the waitress to explain it to him—She thought for a long moment and then proclaimed that it was "a great big old thing". My husband manfully ordered it and sure enough—even by Texas standards it was Huge! And good.

MY FIRST AIRPLANE RIDE

July 31st, 1945!—How can I forget that date—We were finally going to leave Fort Worth to pursue our new life in New York.

It had been a very busy time lately because so many eventful things had already occurred in the last few months, particularly in March when our daughter Nancy was born, and sadly in April, when our wonderful wartime president Roosevelt passed away.

He was the first president I ever voted for and I, and most of our country would sorely miss his Sunday night radio fireside chats and the encouraging words he so skillfully uttered.

Also, thank heavens our war with Germany finally came to a victorious ending and Al and I were looking forward to resuming a more normal future on the east coast.

Luckily because of Al's senior position at Consolidated Vultee we were able to fly from Fort Worth to Washington, D.C. in a private company bomber plane.

I who was deathly afraid of heights because of falling onto the subway tracks when I was 10 years old, was extremely nervous about the flight but hoped that I would somehow overcome my fears once I was on board.

Also the fact that Donald Nelson, the head of the war production board, was flying with us made me feel more comfortable. I knew he was most important in American governmental affairs, so I thought God would keep him safe, and therefore I and my family would literally ride along on his coat tails.

He was really a nice man and said that Nancy was very cute and good on the trip. He also kindly wrote a little message for her on his card, which I still have.

During the flight (which was very smooth), I had to prepare Nancy's lunch, and the stewardess invited me into the kitchen galley to do so. It was fully equipped with a Frigidaire, and an electric stove, so there I was way up in the sky "cooking"! I couldn't believe it. I don't think even Julia Child could match me.

Consequently even though this was my first flight, I deemed it as being extremely memorable and a forerunner of my experiencing many more airplane adventures.

I REMEMBER YOU

Sometimes my early memories become an embarrassment to me. Even though I distinctly remember casual people from way back, these people have no idea who I am. Quel domage!

Here's an example of this ability. A little girl whom I met while summering at a hotel in Asbury Park with my parents, when I was approximately 6 or 7, and whose name I still recall—Janet Jacobson, never crossed my path again until I was about 30 or so (incidentally we have never met since that time).

However, at Atlantic Beach, many years ago, I was sitting on the beach with my very young children, and noticed the profile of a lady sitting near me in the sand.

Somehow I recognized that profile as belonging to my little friend Janet from long ago.

I approached her timidly and asked if she was indeed my little Janet. She responded yes but had absolutely no idea who I was.

I explained that my memory of her included the fact that she had a doll with 7 heads. The body of that doll, could with a slight twist accommodate the head of a dutch child with blonde braids, a Spanish head with black hair containing decorative combs, a French head, and four other heads representing various other countries.

I loved that doll and always wished for one just like it, which unfortunately for me, never happened.

I then told her I recalled that her mother had passed away and subsequently her father had married her mother's sister.

Needless to say, this really caused her to gasp, but of course she still didn't recall ever knowing me.

This is one example of the embarrassment such memories have caused me.

Also the fact that I lived in Palm Beach starting in 1946 and met tons of people at the Palm Beach Hotel and in the Worth Avenue shops, and around the town generally, always brought back many memories of past associations.

But then I moved away for many years and finally when I returned there 7 years ago and met some of the people I knew back then (the few who are still alive) most do not have the vaguest idea that we've ever met.

Therefore I am of the opinion that my long term memory is not a blessing or possibly I'm just not the type of person people remember!

TIME HATH WROUGHT CHANGES

Many years ago a long time friend Rita Fieber and I decided to have a 30 year reunion with the young girls we knew from grade school, High school, and our neighborhood, which in this case was the upper West Side Side of Manhattan—from 72 to 96 Street)

We invited 40 ladies (no longer girls) and we took a general survey of their lives since we last met.

First of all we found that of the 40, 10 had been divorced once, 4 had been divorced twice and one had the honor of being wed 3 times.

The second rather startling discovery was that the former most beautiful one was now chubby, dowdy and not very charming.

The formerly most unattractive person was now beautiful, chic and decidedly sophisticated.

Then of all things, the least affluent one was now sporting a ten carat diamond and seemed to be partial to Chanel from top to toe.

We were all very happy to be together and looked forward to a future reunion.

No doubt, if this reunion takes place 30 years hence, there will be many more changes, that is—if we all survive!

BERNICE ZAKIN

SEEING YOURSELF THROUGH SOMEONE ELSE'S EYES

There she is—Bernice Zakin—I've heard about her. I understand she can be a fairly pleasant person—but not too bright, and certainly not the best bridge player.

I also heard that she lived in many different places. Do you think her parents couldn't pay the rent? Or maybe her family were very noisy and were bad neighbors.

Also there is a rumor that she is very fussy about colors. Everything has to be coordinated in her closets. Maybe that's why she became an interior designer.

Recently someone told me that Bernice only likes people who arrive on time, which certainly rules me out.

Most likely she has many friends, but I'm certainly not one of them, and I have no desire to be.

Besides a good friend of mine told me that Bernice eats a lot and loves pickles. That certainly doesn't define a particularly refined or genteel person.

However if I ever meet her personally, I'll try to be pleasant.

WAS I A GOOD MOTHER?

What a question—what kind of mother would ever admit to having failed maternally.

I personally fully intended to be a perfect mother no sooner had I set eyes upon my beautiful little daughter Nancy, when she was first placed in my arms so long ago in Fort Worth Texas. This was particularly so because I'd thought she'd be a very ugly little boy.

As a child I had gently played with my dolls and kept them clean, nicely dressed and fed regularly, (naturally in an imaginary way), so I certainly felt equipped to handle a real person equally well.

Little did I know that real people, especially teeny ones require a different kind of care.

Nevertheless I believe I managed extremely well for the first 3 years of Nancy's life which incidentally coincided with the birth of my second child (my son Kenny). At that time Nancy developed a very high fever and bad cold and then suddenly stopped eating. when I say "stopped eating", I mean entirely! Not a morsel of food or even liquids would pass her tightly sealed lips.

So of course, as most every well informed mother of that era generally did, I consulted Dr. Spock's book and read the chapter which said "If The Child Refuses To Eat, Don't Worry, Eventually He Or She Will".

However as bright as we thought Nancy was, she was unable to read and therefore had not read Dr. Spock's Book. Consequently after 4 days of no intake of nourishment, my pediatrician felt that she would require hospitalization.

So off she went to be fed intravenously, and sadly my pediatrician would not allow me to visit her, as he felt I was responsible for her refusal to eat due to the arrival of my second child. (Jealously having reared its' ugly head).

Nevertheless I was allowed to visit the hospital every day during this 2 week period and glimpse her through a one way mirror.

Wonder of wonders Nancy was finally discharged from the hospital and arrived home. She told me that she had learned to eat cereal and asparagus, but was not happy as I was the only Mommy who did not come to visit her child in the hospital. You can imagine how I felt about that.

Incidentally that pediatrician wanted me to pay his suit cleaning bill as he bemoaned the fact that Nancy had thrown up on him while he had attempted to feed her. In addition he suggested that I tie her to the breakfast table if she refused to eat anything on her return home, and possibly feed her what she threw up.

As you can readily understand, I considered myself to be a complete failure as a mother for having kept that pediatrician for so long.

And by the way, I was eventually told that the pediatrician's wife had suffered 10 miscarriages, therefore he probably hated other people's kids but mostly Nancy.

EDDIE

The year was 1953 and my husband and I had just moved into our new house in Lawrence, Long Island. The house was not entirely painted, we did not have all of our furniture in place, we had 2 very young children, and very frazzled nerves.

Like a gift from the gods, a neighbor from across the street rang our bell and said the following "we know you must be very tired from moving so we'd love you to come over to our house for a drink".

We were thrilled to comply, and after spending an hour or so with them, a long lasting friendship was established.

Approximately 2 weeks later, our neighbors in the new house next door were about to move in. As we were already acquainted with their in-laws, who had pleaded with us to be kind to their children as they had a little baby and would need helpful neighbors, we were anxious to go the extra mile in order to be very gracious and nice.

Therefore we decided to emulate the Zelinkas, (the nice couple across the street) and so Al, my husband, approached Eddie Rothenstein who was standing next door in his front yard, and invited him and his wife to our house for a drink.

Eddie simply mumbled "no thanks" whereupon Al came back into our house and said "the hell with them".

A few days later I was walking up the street with Selma Zelinka who was wheeling her little son in his carriage. As we passed the Rothenstein house (they had moved in two days previously), there was Eddie's wife in her doorway graciously yelling "hi I'm Shirley—do you want to come in to see our house".

Selma and I were rather nonplussed by Shirley's warm invitation, (I had already told Selma about Eddie's rudeness) but anyway we decided to accept.

We entered the house, which was completely furnished (mind you they had only lived there 2 days). Shirley showed us the interior of her kitchen cabinets, where everything was in perfect order. Next she showed us the insides of her upstairs closets. Every blessed item was neatly arranged and every room resembled a magazine layout. I of course had drop cloths, step ladders and loads of filled cartons in my house.

When I admired something in the kitchen that was especially innovative, Shirley said "Eddie did it. He'll do it for you too if you wish".

I thought to myself "humph—that rude guy would do something for me?"

How wrong I was—After becoming very dear friends with this couple, I learned that Eddie was in a big hurry the day we extended our drink invitation, as he and Shirley had left their baby Barbara back at their old apartment with a housekeeper who had to leave at a particular time. Eddie however, was never one to waste words and therefore declined our overture so abruptly.

Yes—Eddie indeed did many terrific things for us and proved to be a most wonderful friend and neighbor, always loyal, gracious and willing to help others. He was a truly great guy, who unfortunately passed away a few days ago.

We will never forget his many kindnesses, and the wonderful times we spent together throughout those many eventful Lawrence years.

THE 5 TOWNS AND LIDO

Interspaced between our winter months in Palm Beach, Florida from 1946 to 1969, and then Hollywood, Florida for about seven winters, plus an additional twenty winters at the Doral Country Club in Florida, Al and I still managed to raise our children, and lead almost normal lives in Lawrence, Long Island.

Although I must say Al really burnt the candle at both ends. He maintained his office in New York, had shops in Florida at the Palm Beach Hotel, the Hollywood Beach Hotel and the Doral Beach hotel, all at the same time. He did have wonderful sales help in these shops, but of course he had to be "hands on".

In the summer months he was in the New York office until 2 PM each weekday and then drove to the shop at the Lido Hotel in Lido Beach, Long Island, where he worked until midnight every day except Mondays when he could finally relax. The Lido Hotel as well as the Palm Beach Hotel was owned by the Seiden Family. Gladys Sunshine was their daughter and she and husband Morton became our closest friends from 1946 until last year when sadly Gladys passed away and Morton unfortunately is now in a nursing home.

Lido was *the* fashion spot in those early days. They had the wealthiest (mostly Jewish) clientele from all over the country, and they also provided their guests with the best food as well as the most well known theatrical celebrities who performed every Wednesday, Friday and Saturday nights so life there was every glamorous and entertaining.

At the hotel it was necessary to wear formal attire on Wednesday and Saturday nights which were show nights, and cocktail clothes on Friday nights for their Champagne hour, which was when guests who had taken dancing lessons that week would display their dancing abilities with the instructors. It was always a fun evening.

My wardrobe during those years consisted of evening clothes, bathing and golf attire and very little else. Of course off season—September to December I would be able to wear a sweater or blouse with slacks or a skirt. But actually my basic wardrobe consisted of evening clothes. It was very strange indeed and I really relished being in a sweater when I was able to do so. Al actually wore out his tuxedo every season.

From 1953 to 1968 we were members of the Lido Golf Club—That was when the Seiden family purchased and refurbished the old Lido Golf Club. Since Al was a very low handicap player it was very convenient and really most enjoyable for him to play there on a regular basis. I was a novice golfer in 1953 but finally became respectable as the years went by.

Because of the nature of our business and the different places in which we lived during those hotel years, Al and I met hundreds of people, a good number of whom became our very good friends, and it is a rare occasion when I don't know "someone" no matter where I go.

We also met many celebrities along the way—Guy and Carmen Lombardo were long time customers, as was Henry Youngman, Roberta Peters and Judge Samuel Leibowitz. Once Al had a flat tire when delivering a piece of jewelry to the Judge who lived in Brooklyn and he was kind enough to drive Al back to our house in Lawrence at midnight. The car thankfully arrived the next day driven by a garage person. Sam and his wife were lovely people and we thoroughly enjoyed their company. Sid Caesar was a very longtime customer and he and Al also used to spend a lot of social time together during which a lot of vodka was exchanged.

One evening at the Lido Hotel a girl approached Al's showcase while he was placing jewelry in the cases. He didn't bother looking up when she said "my brother sends his regards to you" but Al then said, still looking down "who's your brother?" She answered "Shelly Streisand". Then Al looked up and calmly said "hello Barbra". They both laughed of course and she turned out to be a very lovely person with a beautiful complexion and exquisite hands.

Peter Max's father, Jacob Finkelstein was the pearl merchant from whom Al bought all his pearls therefore we were all very good friends and we were always invited to the birthday parties Peter had for his father. At one party we were seated with Henry Youngman and his wife and Henry said to me "Bernice I know your husband is a jeweler but I want to give you a diamond pin anyway, which he did—It was a dime glued onto a safety pin! I still have it.

Also Milton Berle was a frequent visitor to the Palm Beach Hotel where his mother was usually a guest and she was also a good friend of my mother's. Because of this Milton generally usurped our cabana when he was in town, as his mother was usually there with my mother—consequently Al and I really had no place to sit on those occasions as so many people came over to visit with Milton thinking it was his cabana.

But the celebrity highlight of Palm Beach was always on the occasion of my daughter Nancy's famous birthday parties—Bob Smith "Howdy Doody" always entertained at these events and everyone was so excited to see him (both adults and children). He was a truly great guy. His wife

Mildred and I used to play scrabble together while they were in town (I won't tell you who usually won).

Also Bob once invited Al and I, plus my children to be in his TV peanut gallery and introduced me as beautiful Bernice and Al as awful Al—both adjectives of course were incorrect.

Leslie Nielson who later on became a well known movie star was first married to Monica Boyer, a very talented singer who entertained quite often at Lido. We all became friends and Leslie came to our house one time and spent most of the evening playing games on the floor with Nancy (age 5). Sadly he passed away this year.

Jerry Lewis brought his first wife's engagement ring from Al and many other people of renown usually befriended, played golf with, and purchased jewelry from him so we really had very glamorous associations in those years.

When I recall these occasions I realize how much fun we had and what fond memories I still have.

1967

In 1967 we joined the Woodmere Club which became our home away from home. We knew practically all the members from living locally, and also because so many of the members were our old friends who had stayed at the various hotels in which we had concessions. The Woodmere Club was unique, like a big family—many of the members' children married other members' children so most everyone was related to each other. My daughter Nancy met her present husband Jeff through a member (Carol Weiss) and we will always be grateful to her for that great event.

In those club years everyone had a great time. My golf was good, Al's golf was exceptional, we went to many beautiful parties and had scores of dear friends. Financially our business flourished, and in the country everything was on an even keel. If only things could have stayed the same but of course that was not to be. The French have a favorite saying "plus ça change plus le même chose", but in present day America things always change but *not* for the best, nor do they stay the same so the French don't know everything.

In 1976 my mother whom I dearly loved, passed away. She was a most unusual person able to do anything. She was a fabulous cook and baker, and had a wonderful sense of humor as well. She went to The Columbia University School of Design for 2 years and became a decorator when I was about 9 years old. I guess that is why I wanted to follow in her footsteps. However her career was never extensive as she preferred designing just for friends and family. Big business was never her goal.

Nevertheless at the various hotels we frequented, mostly at the Lido my mother became a star attraction. At the end of each season all of the hotels used to have Masquerade Balls, at which my mother always won first prize for the most original costume. Each costume was always timely and most unusual.

Once she came as the "Kinsey Report". She built a quilted head board which she attached to her waist with a belt. It had a reading light on the top and she wore a little sleeping cap which made her resemble a very old lady. She also put a little pimple on her cheek with hair coming out to indicate age, and pushed a breakfast wagon pleated with the same fabric as the head board with a pair of pantyhose filled with sand so it looked like she was in bed with her legs up. The feet stuck out of the end of the cart and were encased in imitation rubber painted with red toe nail polish. She held the "Kinsey Report" in her arms and had a sign that said "Now he tells me".

Another time she came as "you can't take it with you". She had the local hotel artist paint a black body suit like a skeleton and she shaped an "Easydo" closet in which she walked, that made her look like she was in a coffin. On the side and back of the closet were all the things you can't take with you when you die. There was a 5 carat ring (5 carrots attached to a embroidery hoop), an ermine tail, the sheet music of "you can't take it with you", a toy Rolls Royce, and a roll of fake money.

Another year my mother actually launched the first sputnick at the end of August. (The Russians launched theirs in September). She came in a clear plastic bubble and actually looked like an out of space machine. When people asked her how she came up with the idea before the Russians, she simply said it was "the geophysical year".

She won first prize for her efforts for 12 years in a row and one year a Hollywood mogul who was present offered her a most important costuming job in Hollywood which of course she did not accept.

Besides all that she was just a wonderful person and I was so lucky to have had her as my mother.

My sister Zelma who was 10 years my senior also had a very interesting career as the head of the NY Warner Brothers talent department and my brother-in-law Buddy Kornheiser was head of the Art dept at the same NY Warner office, but they did not meet there. He also lived in the same apartment house that we did, however they did not meet there either. They actually met at a party. Fate is truly strange.

Before she was married Zelma dated Al Hirshfeld the cartoonist and I remember him coming to our house with a red beard and mustache. Bill Hearst Jr. was also a friend of hers. She also briefly dated Nelson Eddy in between his divorces, and Anton Dolan the famous ballet dancer. His original name was Patrick Dolan and he was not gay. One of her most well known theatrical discoveries was Patricia Neal who passed away this year. Zelma was also a judge in the Miss America contest in Atlantic City where Bess Meyerson was crowned Miss America. Incidentally they became very good friends and Bess was very much a member of our family for a while.

When Buddy left Warner Brothers he opened his own art studio and did all the NY commercial artwork for Warner Brothers and United Artists, theatre posters, etc. At one time before Peter Max became "the Peter Max". His father asked Al if Buddy could possibly employ Peter. But at the time Buddy did not need any additional artistic help in his studio. Too bad.

Because of our friendship with the entire Seiden family we were usually sitting with them on Saturday nights during the many celebratory performances. Therefore it was not unusual to be spending the evening with Frank Sinatra, Victor Borge and so many other well known people in the theatrical world.

Both Zelma and Buddy have passed away as has Al, so my immediate family no longer exists.

Thankfully I have wonderful children Nancy and Jeff and Barbi and Kenny as well as 11 grandchildren and 13 great grandchildren. What more can anyone want.

NORTH SHORE TOWERS

Now of course I reside at the North Shore Towers on the North Shore of Long Island. It is an absolutely wonderful place where everything is at my finger trips. A Movie theater, a grocery store, a drugstore, 3 swimming pools, golf and tennis courts and lots of other shops and conveniences. Most of all I have made many many good friends here and with whom I play bridge and canasta. I also spend my winters in Palm Beach which is not at all as wonderful as it was when I lived there in my early years but it is still a pleasant winter vacation spot. Certainly not as great as Arizona.

However when our hotel years came to an end in 1987 we started spending our winters in Arizona which became a most enjoyable period of time. We lived in Scottsdale where the people, food, weather and lifestyle were all wonderful and in addition an unexpected friendship with my formerly unknown cousins Carol and Jay Rosenblatt was a bonus and happily we are still great friends. Carol of course is my only living cousin.

Finally after enjoying many European vacation trips to many different countries through the years, I am probably going to Paris next week for a final time—I believe it will be my 8th time there. When I get home I'll be ready to sit back and start writing about my past trips and since I've kept very complete diaries of my first 12 trips to Europe I believe I have enough material to rediscover these places in print.

AU REVOIR!

THE NEVERS IN MY LIFE

I've never had a hamburger
I only eat hot dogs without a roll
I've never had ketchup
I never use ice cubes
I never eat dark chocolate candy or cake
I never eat bagels
I order chicken chow mein without the chicken
(I simply like the chicken flavor)
I won't eat frosting on cake
I avoid anything that contains the number seven
I won't eat a doughnut
I admit to being peculiar
If I don't like what a thing looks like I won't eat it
On the other hand if I don't do any of the above
I can *never* say I *don't* do them!

I PROMISED TO KEEP IT A SECRET

Years ago I had a neighbor who told me a deep dark secret—her sister and brother-in-law were on the verge of divorce and no one was supposed to know because it might involve a rather nasty public disclosure of unfortunate events.

Being a very naïve and honorable person (which I presumably was) I sealed my lips, crossed my fingers and hoped to leave this world forever if I revealed a word of this incident to anyone.

Some weeks later several people at different times whispered this secret information to me—and I was truly confused—who had disclosed what was supposedly unknown?.

At that point I told my neighbor what had happened and her unexpected response was—oh I told everyone and besides I never thought you would really keep it a secret.

So much for good intentions.

A HORSE OF ANOTHER COLOR

My husband who was in the jewelry business had many wealthy customers, and fortunately for us, they loved luxury possessions, and as a consequence, they all became our frequent jewelry purchasers.

On occasion though, some of the affluence of these people had a way of diminishing.

One time a particularly well monetarily positioned person (or so we thought) had dreadful financial reversals. He owed my husband a sizeable sum of money, and the only way he was able to make a payment on his debt, was to give my husband one of his racehorses.

Neither my husband nor myself were racetrack enthusiasts and we could hardly make head or tail (forgive the pun) out of our new possession, so we put the horse up for sale.

We were lucky enough to find a buyer very quickly, even tho we had to take a financial loss.

At the time, this incident was printed on the front page of the New York Times and unfortunately for us, the following year we read that the horse came in first at the Belmont Raceway and Kentucky Derby, which awarded the new owner a very tidy sum.

Former owners of course get nothing.

THE TABLE OF CONTENTS

I was always known for my kitchen prowess and beautiful dinner parties, and certainly took great pains to entice my guests with an array of tempting edibles.

At any rate one evening, many years ago I invited 12 people to my home for a dinner party and I believe they were eagerly anticipating the taste of my legendary cookery.

Everything was ready on time, the menu was fabulous, the dining room table looked divine, and I was delighted to be the talented hostess.

After a leisurely cocktail hour, my flushed and jolly guests, tipsily entered the dining room for our first course, which was delicious.

Then our entreés were served and just when we had all started eating, one of our guests began telling an interesting story.

He became increasingly vocal, no doubt due to the many drinks he had consumed, and suddenly banged on the table to make a point.

To make a long story short, the entire bottom of the table collapsed, the dishes and their contents swayed and finally flew to the carpeting, the dinner vanished and my guests were left without food.

Luckily there was a nearby delicatessen so we all went there for sandwiches.

THE RED LEATHER DIARY

In the early 60's, when my husband Al and I were eagerly contemplating our first post war trip to Europe, it was considered to be a very novel adventure.

All our friends were enthusiastic for us and several banded together to have a series of luncheons for me which included the presentation of lovely farewell gifts.

At one of these functions I was pleased to receive a beautiful red leather diary, in which I could presumably enter all exciting items relating to the several cities we intended to visit.

With much anticipation we boarded the plane in New York and leaned back in our seats.

I had my little red diary in my lap because I wanted to write every thrilling event of the trip starting with the flight itself, while my husband thought he'd catch up reading the news of the day in the New York Times.

However as he leaned back the seat collapsed and he found himself on the floor.

A solicitous stewardess quickly arrived and said my husband would have to move up to First Class as there were no other seats available in our part of the plane. Actually this would have been a treat for Al since it was his birthday.

Al said he really couldn't leave his wife and could I possibly come with him but the stewardess stood her ground and said there was only one seat left up front. Gallantly Al offered me his new space but as it was his natal day, I refused. So there I was all alone in my section eating the bland fixings to which my seat was entitled. while Al on the other hand was feasting on numerous portions of caviar in his luxurious accommodations.

Thankfully my nice little red diary was available, and I was able to enter the details of this woeful situation and experience of my first European adventure, and I still vividly remember having much jealously and hunger pangs.

THEY "TRIPPED" UP

During the 70's my husband and I were going to Greece with another couple. We were all good friends and anticipated having a wonderful time together.

Plans were enthusiastically arranged for restaurant dining and reservations were made. Also, side trips we intended taking out of Athens (which was to be our first stop) were also well thought out, and we really couldn't wait to visit the exciting historical sites we knew we expected to see.

Since we had hired a station wagon to pick up our friends, and ourselves, along with the many pieces of luggage (which in those days was acceptable by airlines), we were ready when the driver arrived and were all soon enroute to Kennedy Airport.

Halfway there, my husband jokingly said to the other couple, "I'm sure you all have plenty of money and your passports!"

Our friend's wife, after searching frantically in her handbag, sadly announced that she had indeed forgotten her passport.

I must say her husband was most kind and did not get upset, although I think my husband would have killed *me*.

At any rate, we had to turn around and go back to their house. Then after a 15 minute wait during which she could not find her passport, my husband, who was slightly livid by this time, (since we had very little time left before the plane was to depart), yelled out "hurry up or we will miss the plane".

This didn't help the situation, so we finally had to leave them, and barely got to the plane on time ourselves.

They came to Athens the next day, and her husband was still very calm.

I wish I knew her secret

BARBI AND KEN

Just about every mother of a little girl is familiar with Barbi and Ken dolls.

They were and probably still are, among the favorite playthings of the 5 to 8 year old girl group.

These dolls are distinguished by their enormous collection of clothing and other items, such as beds, houses, jewelry, etc.

As a result, most little girls thoroughly enjoy imaginary lifestyle moments with these dolls, which then become "poignant permanent memories".

Believe it or not, I too have a Barbi and Ken—However mine are real flesh and blood. You see I have a son Ken who is married to a Barbi (she's a doll—but not in the Mattel sense).

But now I have a particular incident concerning *my* Barbi that I would like to relate, and you will probably think that I consider this to be as important of a memory as the ones cited above.

To get to the point—when Barbi and my son married, she said to me "I love you, and will love you forever". I wisely answered "Barbi tell me that again in ten years".

Ten years later—to the day—Barbi wrote me a little note in which she said "I still love you". I was thoroughly flattered and was pleased to consider myself to have been a successful mother-in-law.

That statement, I must admit, was 20 years ago—my son Ken and his Barbi have now been married almost 30 years and since that letter 20 years ago, she has not written me again!

Am I a failure?

TELLING YOUR CHILDREN HOW TO RAISE THEIR CHILDREN

Do I dare to express my opinions about anything, least of all advice to my children (daughter and son) regarding their offspring. Actually I am extremely able to do so, since my children were absolutely perfect, due to my remarkable abilities as their mother.

My daughter, I must admit is a pretty good mother (after all she has my genes). However she always allowed her children to have Twinkies, Oreos and other dietary no nos, which permission (being that I was raised on graham crackers and social teas) I found to be rather unconscionable.

My son, on the other hand has a wife. Now I know his wife exists because I speak to her frequently and dearly love her, however there are so many toys and games, etc in their home that it is not always possible to find *her* or their *children*.

In any case I believe both of these families think I am a fine grandparent providing I don't impose my opinions on them.

Actually I really don't find the need to do so, as their kids are all really great. (Again—they have my genes!)

CAREER BOUND

Ironically in my adulthood I became very friendly with 2 cousins on my father's side and actually worked for one of his sisters, my Aunt Belle Lenert, for ten years. She was a well known interior designer, and since it had always been a dream of mine to enter this field, I was quite elated when she called me out of the blue, just before I graduated from the New York School of Interior Design, and asked if it would be "beneath my dignity" to do a few little things for her. We had met in the street one day so she knew I was pursuing a career in that industry. I grew to love her dearly and was blessed to have learned so much during my assistant years with her. Belle was a remarkable woman, she had many friends in the various fields of the arts, opera, music, etc. and on most Friday afternoons she conducted what probably would be called a "Salon Afternoon" when all these famous people would come to her home for tea and wonderful conversation—lucky me to be there.

Belle had a very beautiful voice and at one time seriously considered having an operatic career. She actually had a successful interview with Giovani Martinelli of Opera fame, but when he asked her if she wanted to get married (not to him of course) or have a life in the opera world, she chose marriage.

After Belle died in the late 70's I went into business for myself and was fortunate enough to inherit all of her wonderful sources and most of her clientele.

I must say my working years (approximately) 35 or so years as an interior designer were quite an exciting period in my life. I had lovely clients. I never had an item returned or not accepted and everyone for whom I designed was usually extremely satisfied. I believe I had about 300 or more clients during these years, so I was either very lucky or they were all just nice people. Best of all I always had the complete respect from my sources and work people.

OFF TO THE SOUTHWEST

During the 20 year period from 1985 to 2005 Al and I spent our winter months in Scottsdale, Arizona.

I had a childhood friend Elaine Kramer who lived there and who had always invited us to visit her, so we finally did. I had introduced her to her first husband and was the godmother of her son. Incidentally because of my visit to Chicago to see her little baby, my cousin in Peoria persuaded me to come to Peoria which was so close to Chicago, and that's how I met Al. Fate is most remarkable.

At any rate on our first trip to Scottsdale while glancing through the "Places To Visit" book in our hotel room at the Boulders (the most terrific place), I noticed the name "Artistic Gallery" on the first page, and at the very top were the names Carole and Jay Rosenblatt, owners.

It occurred to me that she could possibly be my cousin (the daughter of my father's brother), whom I had met just once before, so we called and asked the gallery assistant if the Rosenblatt's (they were in California at the time) were from New York, had 2 children and if Mr. Rosenblatt had previously been in the insurance business. That is all I knew about them.

So when the young lady said yes, we also said "if they think they are our cousins please have them call us at our hotel when they return from LA".

They did—and we have been very close and have enjoyed a wonderful friendship ever since.

As we spent so many winters in Scottsdale, having a real cousin nearby at that time was indeed delightful, and we had great times together.

It is really strange, that my association with members of my father's family, namely Belle, Carole, as well as Belle's 2 daughters, became truly terrific, whereas my mother's family have all died or dispersed to parts unknown and I lost contact with most of them many years ago.

Of course I no longer go to Scottsdale, but Carole and I constantly keep in touch either via telephone, e-mail or when they occasionally come to New York.

So even though I no longer have any aunts or uncles and just a few cousins, my immediate family has certainly expanded. I have 7 grandchildren including 5 married grandchildren, plus their husbands and wives, and 13 great grandchildren—(I inherited some, but still consider all of them as being mine).

THE END OF THE WORLD

On my first visit to Scottsdale, Arizona, I thought I had reached the end of the world. It was so barren, just miles and miles of desert, loads of cacti, tall majestic saguaros, and the unusual jumping cholla, which was a beautiful fuzzy, light green clump that you simply had to touch.

However, if you did, it would immediately attack with needle like spears that jumped right at you, hence the name.

My husband and I were there for the famous golf courses, many of which had an abundant amount of gloriously colored flowers, lush greens, occasional coyotes, lots of rabbits, and such clear cloudless skies that it was easy to think of this place as paradise.

And because the air was so light our golf balls flew extremely far and we could possibly make Tiger Woods jealous.

Originally we stayed in hotels but after a few trips decided it was time for more permanent lodgings. This was 25 years ago when new and spectacular homes were just being built around the various golf courses, and gobbling up the barren desert at the same time.

Most of these houses had huge rooms with ceilings about 20 to 25ft high with bright sunshine filtering thru the spacious rooms.

The kitchens were extremely well planned and had family rooms attached, an excitingly innovative idea at the time. Believe it or not, the front yards all had lovely green grass and various tall trees including palms. Who said there is no green in Arizona?

At any rate, we did not purchase one of the more glamorous homes, which by the way only cost around $200,000 at the time, including a swimming pool and 4 enormous bathrooms with walk-in closets contained therein.

We did however find a lovely ranch at the end of a cul de sac, on our favorite golf course at the Gainey Ranch, and with 20ft ceilings.

The cul de sac which faced our house had a very tall palm tree in the center with varying colored flowers surrounding it. A welcoming sight when we entered our driveway.

The most wonderful part of the house was the neighbors. We met so many great people from all over the U.S., London and Canada who fortunately remain good friends to this day.

It was a close knit group which socialized on a regular basis. In fact once a season our neighbors at the end of the street had a block party to which we all brought delicious homemade edibles, and had great fun. Their house faced the West, as did ours, and the sunsets were incredible, lavender, pink, aqua, bright blue, and yellow—no clouds. Just one wondrous sight after another, which made those evenings unforgettable. It was small town neighborliness—and terrific.

Ours was a manned, gated community with a small common mail building at the gate with grapefruit and orange trees (that had paintted white trunks) lining the three streets of the community, complimented by a swimming pool accessible to all.

Of course we never had to buy our oranges or grapefruits and always chatted with friends at the mail house.

There was also a community club house midway around the golf course, where we played Bridge, had arranged trips to museums, attended book reviews, and enjoyed listening to the many visiting noteworthy speakers. There was also a library attached to the building. The outdoor barbecues were frequent, and since the club house had a baby grand piano, some of the talented neighbors usually entertained us with delightful melodies.

An old fashioned croquet court also existed where everyone wore white and it was reminiscent of a Scott Fitzgerald book, which added to the charm.

The Scottsdale area also had many terrific restaurants with delicious food and at most moderate prices. So we actually had 40 or 50 places where we ate on a regular basis. No wonder we all gained weight, but we did so happily, I might add.

Altho I've never been back, I've had numerous invitations to visit. In the meantime I often do a bit of wistful sighing as I retrace those wonderful years and treasured memories.

2ND TIME AROUND

One winter in the late 1990's while my husband Al and I were spending our usual winter in Scottsdale Arizona, my daughter Nancy and her husband called us and invited the two of us plus my cousin Carole and her husband Jay also from Arizona, to go to Las Vegas for the weekend. She said that my granddaughter Lizzie and her fiancé plus another friend of Lizzie's would be joining us.

This sounded like fun since none of us with the exception of Carole and Jay, had ever been to Las Vegas. In the course of conversation concerning our planned activities for the upcoming weekend, Nancy asked "would you and Dad like to renew your vows".

This kind of took me by surprise but I said I'd have to ask her father—you see we had already been married for over 50 years and I wasn't sure he wanted a further commitment.

Surprisingly he acquiesced—maybe he was afraid to say no, at any rate plans were made for the ceremony at Elvis Presley's Graceland Chapel. Then a friend from New York who manufactured wedding tulle generously sent me 10 yards of it for a veil and train.

We arrived in Las Vegas after a short flight and found out exactly what this wedding entailed. It was to be what is known as a "package deal", everything was included—a white stretch limo to take all of us to and from the

Chapel—a red rose for each person to carry when walking down the aisle, a bouquet of flowers for me, which I discovered consisted of orange, purple and red straggly and wilted posies. A top hat for Al was also provided as well as an authentically attired Elvis to perform the service. Music was to be included, and we would also receive a video of the "happening".

The moment arrived and we solemnly entered the chapel, but were hardly able to suppress our laughter, as we really all looked awful.

I was attired in white golf pants, a light blue cashmere cardigan, and encased in my enormous nine yard tulle train. The remaining one yard Nancy managed to bunch up onto a rather unattractive head piece for me.

Al wore blue golf pants, a shirt and tie plus his borrowed top hat.

The remaining members of the wedding party were attired in blue jeans, white tee shirts and sneakers. Naturally they all carried their red roses when walking down the aisle.

Elvis, or his counterpart performed a rather hilarious ceremony. I had a cigar band for a wedding ring and thank god Al said "I do", although I think he had moments of indecision.

Elvis then got down on his knees and sang "Blue Suede Shoes" to the two of us.

We had no people sitting in the chapel because the entire group walked down the aisle.

I must say I thoroughly enjoyed getting married again, even to the same person (I hope he did).

IS THERE ANYBODY OUT THERE?

A terrible thing occurred recently and I don't believe there is a solution to this situation.

My children and their families recently invited me to dinner at a lovely restaurant, and so I arrived there nicely dressed and was eagerly looking forward to a pleasant evening.

However, after we all profusely greeted each other, we placed our dinner orders, and then my children and their spouses disappeared. Absolutely gone!—well not absolutely—only their faces—their bodies remained and there seemed to be a bit of movement in what might have been their hands.

But they really weren't there—I was totally alone, I hadn't eaten anything and was hungry.

After a while I realized that I was a victim of the "modern age".

They were all texting and I was left alone in the last century!

ELLIE—POIGNANT DETAILS ABOUT HER DEATH

My dearest friend Ellie was dying. She knew this—as did most of her family and friends—but no one would acknowledge the sad and inevitable truth.

"I can't talk to anyone" she said, "no one will listen"—I told her I would and for a while she was able to feel the comfort of those conversations.

Finally, when Ellie passed away—everyone at the funeral *despaired* emotionally—Many tears were shed, hugs were exchanged, and sad groups huddled together for a long time, and then promised to meet and reminisce about Ellie.

If only they had done this before she died!

LOOKING THROUGH OLD ALBUMS AND SCRAP BOOKS

Looking through an old collection of things from childhood during one's mature years can be a wonderful treat, especially on a rainy day. All sorts of delightful items can emerge from yesteryear and many a chuckle can occur as a result.

On one such day I found my autograph album from grade school along with a scrapbook from my early teens.

In the album were all the cute little rhymes students used to write to each other upon graduation, such as "I wish you much, I wish you mighty, I wish your pajamas were next to my nighty. This was considered to be very daring in those days, but today of course 4 letter words would be the norm.

My scrapbook was indeed nostalgia at its prime. There were dried corsages from unremembered boyfriends, an old leaf I picked from a tree at Yale University. It was originally bright red, and now a burnished mahogany color.

There were also Valentines declaring love forever from other old boyfriends who are probably all dead, as well as newspaper items that were sensational in their day.

Among these clippings was the sad story about the Lindbergh baby's kidnapping, and subsequent demise, Gloria Vanderbilt's heartfelt tale involving her aunt's fight for her custody. Who know she'd become such a talented artist and designer as well as the mother of Anderson Cooper the journalist.

The pages bulged with memorabilia and I definitely recommend the keeping of all this Rubbish (which it actually is), as it certainly helps to preserve the wonderful memories of one's youth.

WHO WOULD COME TO MY FUNERAL?

If I had passed away it might have been a very cold blustery day with the possibility of an imminent snowstorm.

Ordinarily on such a day most people might be content to stay home, drink hot chocolate and cozy up with a good book, and snuggle under a warm throw.

However, an obituary notice in the New York Times (which is not easily found these days) most likely would have announced the demise of one Bernice Zakin—me.

At that time, I probably would have been ensconced neatly in my luxuriously lined coffin, dressed to the nines in a glamorous gown (which I might have previously worn at a wedding) and made up to be exotically beautiful.

My numerous relatives and friends would be deeply saddened to realize that such a special person (again—me) had passed away and thus would be anxious to attend my services.

I, in my coffin would be positive that both flattering and tearful eulogies would be made, recalling all my wondrous qualities and great accomplishments. Lamentations that I would be greatly missed would also be made by many attendees.

Alas! This was probably not to be.

No doubt the snowstorm could easily have become a blizzard, preventing anyone coming to the funeral chapel.

What an unfortunate ending that would be to my very eventful life.

It's sad to think that my family and old friends might have preferred hot chocolate as an alternative to bidding me farewell, and that as a result I would be left alone in my coffin and definitely not even able to read a good book.

NEVER GO BACK

Would I ever want to be young again
Certainly not today
Why would I even contemplate
Childhood games to play?

Schooldays hold no brief for me
Who'd ever yearn to do sums
My elderly school marms I've never missed
Nor even my bygone chums.

As for my dates—the boys that I knew
Some were great fun, I must say
But most of them now I'd completely ignore
(No doubt they may have been gay!)

Therefore when I think of my present life
I'm happy, content and at ease
I wouldn't trade it or even go back
Because *now* I do as I please!

AH YOUTH!

Why would I ever want to be young again? It would be a terrible choice—first of all my present wardrobe would not be suitable and it would cost a fortune to buy a young person's clothing.

Secondly, I would probably not have any of my current *grandchildren* and maybe not even the *children* I have now.

Thirdly, I would have to associate with some people who thank god are now dead, (not that I wished them ill at anytime in the past).

Also I would no doubt have to travel by train to get to Florida or Arizona, and it would take forever.

However the only really good things about being young again would be that my husband would still be alive, and I would no longer be allergic to shrimp.

GONE BUT NOT FORGOTTEN

With the advent of the 21st century, I suddenly realized that in my growing up years in the 20th century, many things I previously took for granted were no longer available, or even recognizable to anyone under the age of 50.

I decided to make a list of these items so that I would always be able to recall them with nostalgia.

Here it is:

Grade School Items
a pencil box with compartments housing a pink eraser, a pen holder, pen points, a ruler and #2 pencils with a pencil sharpener. There was a zipper all around this grey marbleized box.

Grade School Rooms
Inkwells, and a person who filled them with ink (fountain pens came later). There was a sewing class, cooking class, music appreciation on Fridays and art appreciation on any day.

School Day Candy Store Purchases
Penny candy such as colored chocolate balls that changed colors each time you took one out of your mouth, long white papers with varicolored candy dots, little tin dishes with a tiny spoon so that you could eat the gooey substance contained within the dish, bubble gum and various other goodies.

Brown paper covers you had to use for the new books that the school provided free of charge.

Games
Roller Skates with 4 wheels and a skate key, a horserein, "pin the tail on the donkey" at birthday parties, potsy, a pink rubber bouncing ball for throwing against a ledge on a building, or playing "123 alery just like a chocolate fairy", jump ropes with various ditties that were recited while jumping.

Clothing
Silk stockings, long underwear, garter belts, woolies, button hooks, bobby pins, hair pins, leggings, corset covers, corsets.

Household Items
2 cent stamps, the milk man, the ice man, penny postcards, the ice box, wash tubs, the egg man who delivered eggs with double yolks, the doctor who came to the house for $5.00 with a little black bag, the knifeman who came to sharpen knives, matches to turn on the oven pilot light, carpet sweepers, dumb waiters, bread boxes, scrubbing boards, moth balls, ice bags, hot water bottles, iodine, argerol, electric fans, toasters with 4 sloping sides to put on top of the stove, slip covers, cash registers.

Stores
McCreerys, Arnold Constable, B. Altman, Orbachs, Bonwit Teller, De Pinnas, Childs, Schraafts, Tip Toe Inn, Horn and Hardart Automat.

Miscellaneous
Butter sold in big tubs by the pound, 3rd and 2nd Ave elevated trains, trolley cars, telegrams, switch boards, Pitman & Gregg secretarial skills

A BEAUTIFUL SPOT—BUT

The evening was absolutely breathtaking as was fairly usual in Scottsdale, Arizona that time of year. It was balmy and a magnificent sunset was resting on the horizon in aquas, pinks and lavenders all blending together in a wonderful mélange of colors.

This was a truly fantastic spot for dining outdoors—and four of us anticipated a fun evening.

A lavish dinner had been ordered, and the first course arrived in all its glory. It was jellied madrilène with shiny black caviar and a dollop of sour cream atop its glistening quiver of tomato.

I gracefully dipped a spoon into my cup and delivered the contents to my lips. Suddenly I was conscious of an unusual substance in my mouth.

I immediately spit it out and realized it was a set of keys on a string. Glaringly I displayed it to the waiter fully expecting an apologetic response. Instead he thanked me profusely for finding them. He further explained that they were the keys to the refrigerator and that he had been searching for them all day.

No—we did not get a free dinner but it was a really interesting experience.

NO HEAT

A few days ago I had a call from a worried friend who lives in Scottsdale, Arizona. She inquiring about my ability to stay warm, because she heard we were having a bit of a chill in Palm Beach.

"I'm absolutely fine" I told her. But then she asked about the funny noise on my telephone—I said "don't worry, it's just my teeth chattering".

"Oh my god" she yelled—are you that cold?—I answered truthfully—"I'm not cold—I'm freezing!"

"Freezing" she gasped—"what are you doing about it?" Well I tried to reassure her that my cashmere lined gloves which I thoughtfully wore travelling from New York in December, were snuggly on my finger tips.

I also had my lap and legs covered with a nice woolen blanket, there was a cup of hot tea right next to me on a table, and other than the fact that my nose was ice cold and running profusely, and that I no longer felt my ears, everything else seemed to be in order, and that I could actually move my tongue.

Aghast, she then asked "don't you have heat in your apartment?" Of course I told her. "I certainly do", "except that it isn't working, and it's Sunday so nobody can come to fix it, besides all the people who are on emergency shifts are home trying to keep warm".

My good friend then vehemently demanded to know the exact temperature in my apartment—I told her I would be happy to give her that information except that I was unable to open my terrace door as it was frozen shut and that was where I had the thermometer.

"Oh you poor thing" she moaned—"what are your plans for the day?"—I explained that I had already contacted the cryonics people, advising them not to pick me up to place in one of their machines because I had my own nice "frozen in time" position right where I was sitting.

My alternative to the Cryonics people was a full bottle of wine at the ready, with hopes for a warm and tipsy future.

I also don't remember who said "if winter comes—can spring be far behind", but I certainly hope it proves to be true this year.

THE TRIP WOULD BE PUNISHING

This past October I was looking forward to a lovely day driving through the countryside, particularly to admire the golden, russet and scarlet tones of the crisp fall leaves, still clinging to the multiple branches of the trees along the parkway.

It was a day I had planned for several weeks, and when the morning finally arrived, I couldn't have been more excited.

However, I did not anticipate the sudden change in the weather pattern, which took place halfway to my destination, namely a fairly well known restaurant, nestled in the woods, and boasting a magnificent view of the varicolored mountains.

I was almost there when a downpour of enormous force came down from the heavens, making it impossible to continue driving, and also made it quite hazardous to stop on the side of the road.

At my own peril, however I endeavored to continue driving, but to no avail.

I finally had to stop on the roadside, which I could barely see, and ate the apple that I had brought along as a "just in case".

I sat there for almost 3 hours, then finally turned back to return home, as it was too late to continue towards the restaurant.

Who knew this trip would be so punishing.

A MEAL SURREAL

There it was in all its glory! The most beautiful display of beautiful food that I had ever seen.

Mountains of pink glistening oversized shrimp, piled high on crushed ice in an ornate silver bowl, luscious red Maine lobsters artistically arranged on a lovely scalloped antique tray, fried chicken pieces with an apparent crispiness, so that I could almost hear the crunch, and because the pieces were so enticingly displayed, they were impossible to resist.

There were also enormous white vividly colored green asparagus that practically beckoned everyone passing by to take some.

The numerous salads with varying greens, and the unusually shaped vegetables surrounding the quivering aspics drew me into a world of color.

In addition the many varieties of fresh fruits that seemed to be bursting with flavor with a far reaching pungent aroma as well, made a wonderful addition to the glorious buffet table.

Then at last a parade of at least 25 cakes of all kinds—so divine in their whipped cream and chocolate finery, meringues and fruit filled tarts, plus a myriad of colorful decorated cookies.

Everything was so tempting, it was difficult to refrain from filling my plate completely, and possibly contemplating second or more portions.

Unfortunately however, I realized that I was actually having a dream, and that the magnificence before me didn't really exist, but even tho I was conscious that I was dreaming, and that many people around me were eating ravenously, I didn't seem able to fill a plate of my own.

I think it was my birthday because all the people present were greeting and congratulating me effusively, and we were having lengthy conversations. Consequently time passed very quickly without my ever being able to fill my empty plate.

I was finally able to take a sizeable slice of fabulously decorated lemon custard cake (my true favorite) which I seemed to devour and enjoy to the utmost.

Then I cut a piece of scrumptious looking strawberry shortcake and tried to put *that* on my plate, but it kept sliding off and every time I tried to take a bite it fell from my fork and finally landed on the floor.

Just at that moment I awakened—practically starving and then it hit me! How stupid!—In my sudden departure from my dream I completely forgot to get the name of the very talented caterer!

MY INHERITANCE

Recently I received a letter in which I was informed that a cousin of mine had passed away, leaving a will wherein I was named as his last remaining relative and beneficiary.

This was a most surprising bit of information as I had not known of his existence.

In fact, I had never even met his father, who was my father's youngest brother.

His father whose name was Samuel had lived in California most of his adult years and therefore my father who lived in New York, rarely had any contact with him. I don't believe any other members of the family had contact either. Certainly no one even knew he had a son.

How this cousin knew my name was extremely puzzling. Maybe the internet was his source.

Nevertheless the will stipulated that he had named a particular male friend (most likely gay) to inherit the bulk of his estate, but no amount was mentioned.

I however was to receive a small stipend with the proviso that I sign my willingness to forego any claims to the estate.

My stipend was to be the grand sum of $1.00. At last I was an heiress!

At first I thought this whole situation was a scam, but after receiving several letters (which I had originally ignored), I was finally served with a summons.

This summons stated that I had to be in a Dallas courtroom at 9 AM, in approximately one week, or else sign the papers that were presented in the summons.

Not wanting to go to Texas, I decided to sign.

Then I was curious to know something about this unknown cousin. I tried calling the number listed for his heir, but to no avail. There was never any answer indicating someone was home so I finally gave up.

The entire incident probably would have been finalized except for one thing.

I have yet to receive my $1.00.

After all, I was a blood relative and an heiress so I'm certainly entitled to my full share.

The unknown person who most likely received millions of dollars because of my signature is no doubt enjoying life on the French Riviera tooling around in his new Rolls Royce, and entertaining royalty in his enormous chateau—I on the other hand am still patiently waiting at my mail box everyday in hopes of receiving my inheritance.

BLING

The other day I was on the 3rd Avenue Bus in New York and noticed that the lady opposite me was wearing what appeared to be a very worn pair of blue jeans with tattered holes in both knees.

She was also sporting a shiny diamond ring which I judged to be approximately 10 carats. Wow! I thought to myself—that is huge! But then again I couldn't imagine that anyone in such decrepit jeans would be wearing such an ostentatious diamond on a public conveyance (that is, if the stone was genuine).

Of course I understand that today holey jeans are quite fashionable and expensive (although not in a religious sense), but even if the person wearing them was rich or poor, such a flashy bauble did not seem to be appropriate on a public bus.

Perhaps the stone was not genuine, in that case the owner could possibly be accosted and robbed by a felon, who did *not* know the difference between faux and real.

At any rate if the diamond was the *real thing*, it certainly made a statement about the wearer's financial status, despite the old jeans.

However if it was *not* an authentic stone then I'm surely going to try buying a similar one at my beauty parlor boutique.

YOUNG AT HEART

When my grandson became engaged some years ago my daughter had a beautiful party for the young couple, at which I was seated at a table with the bride to be's grandparents.

Her grandmother told me she thought my grandson was charming and good looking, and then she queried "do you have any other grandsons". I said yes, I do have one more. Then she asked "is he married". I informed her that he was still single. She finally asked "do you think he might be getting married soon".

At this time I was forced to explain that my unmarried grandson was very short, had no money, no job and still lived at home with his parents.

I believe she was quite disheartened by this information, until I told her that he was only twelve years old!

MY QUANDARY

I wake up sometimes during the night and think that I'm *thinking*, and then I feel compelled to write about what I'm *thinking*—but then, if I have trouble falling asleep again after I get through *thinking* about what I'm *thinking*, and if I'm still awake after I finally write about what I've been *thinking*, then I have to write about *something else* while I'm still awake.

But even if I take a sleeping pill so that I can fall asleep, and not have to write *anything* (because I only write when I can't sleep), there is a problem since I hate to take pills.

All in all it's a vicious cycle—and I'm *thinking* (because I'm awake) that I should write *something* anyway so that maybe I can fall asleep after I finish writing about what I'm *thinking*—or at least try to sleep.

NY TIMES OBITS

Lately I seem to register complaints about many people and things, but in the following particular case, I believe I am completely justified, I would therefore like to explain said justification.

In re: The New York Times—this venerable publication, to which I have been a loyal and paying customer for more years than I can presently remember, has a new arrangement.

Since their so called austerity endeavor, they have taken their obituary page away from the back of the first section, and placed it in strange and unusual places within the paper. As for instance—first, it appeared in the Business Section, which I can almost understand, as death is really Big Business.

But, then after weeks of futile attempts to find my dead people, there they were in the Arts Section, right next to the crossword puzzle no less. Is there a connection do you suppose? Like—"What's a common word for a stiff older person?" But now, just last Sunday I discovered a real tragedy. My dead people are now in the Sports Section. This is the one I usually throw away before reading. (Is death now the new Game in town?")

What to do? I'll tell you what *I* had to do—I had to fish that section out of the garbage just to find out who died this week!

It so happened I did not know any of the listed people. But what if I did know any of the names? Then I would have missed commiserating with many families regarding lost loved ones. I would not have sent memorial donations to honor them, thus cutting off monetary gains for worthwhile charities.

I might also have missed some funerals, thereby not using gas in my car and possibly eliminating income from Libya (not that I care about that) and in general irritating me to no end.

I believe, as such an old (I *do* mean old) customer of the New York Times, that I am entitled to find my dead people easily. I don't mind searching for the Metropolitan Diary because that only appears once a week. But seven days of searching for obituaries is really too much to ask of any old and live person.

It's like asking "Where's Waldo?"

IMPORTANT NOTICE ON J DATE

Hereby is a list of attributes which exemplify the following Jewish person "Me".

1. I'm short or tall enough for any sized gentleman

2. I'm slim enough to fit into a size 8, and yet interested enough in food to cook for a nice Jewish date.

3. I play a decent game of Bridge and any other games most gentlemen enjoy.

4. I love the idea of having in-laws come to visit, even beyond the usual 3 days.

5. If a gentleman has children, I will be more than happy to gather them unto my bosom, which is quite ample.

6. He does not have to be "well to do" as long as he "does well".

7. I enjoy getting up early in order to prepare a delicious breakfast such as French toast or pancakes. I can also make Matzo Brei at Passover

8. This gentleman does not have to open the door when I get out of his car, although it would be nice if he *had* a car.

9. I am most willing to be an active member of his temple, even if it means walking 3 miles in sneakers on Yom Kippur.

10. I do not speak Yiddish but am willing to learn.

11. Je suis tres charmante—Shalom!

WHAT A GREAT DINNER

The other evening I was with 4 good friends at a wonderful and expensive restaurant. Since we were all in the mood for a sumptuous repast to celebrate the birthday of one of the group, we all ordered extravagantly.

As the birthday person was my dearest friend, I intended to play hostess, and was therefore paying for each person's dinner. Everyone was in accord that I should order the same items for all. So the first thing I ordered was 3 bottles of very good champagne from a vintage year.

The first course was a delicious salad with avocados, artichoke hearts, heirloom tomatoes, hearts of palm, 4 kinds of greens and a marvelous green goddess dressing, which naturally included some anchovies—imported of course.

Then came clams casinos which absolutely melted in our mouths. By the way, the champagne had already been freely poured and was imbibed very enthusiastically and continuously.

For our entrée we had rare roast beef au jus, twice stuffed and cheese covered baked potatoes, soufled spinach, creamed mushrooms with delicate spices, and candied carrots.

The many desserts included crème bruleé, strawberry shortcake, and French macaroons. Both lemon and chocolate soufflés, Italian cheesecake and varied chocolate covered fruits, such as apricots, strawberries and pineapple were also served.

We each consumed some of everything with great relish and after downing an after dinner liqueur, everyone concluded that this dinner was absolutely beyond compare.

The appropriate number of candles had already been inserted in the strawberry shortcake to honor the birthday girl, and then our waiters as well as several other restaurant guests, all chimed in with us when we sang a very off key "Happy Birthday".

All in all this evening was unanimously voted to be "wonderbar" and I proudly presented my credit card to the waiter with aplomb.

Unfortunately my card was denied as I was apparently over my limit.

What a dire situation! Thankfully the manager allowed us to leave after I guaranteed that I would return the next day with another card or cash.

Incidentally the next day I threw up!

MAIL

Today I received a most disturbing letter. Included in the envelope there was a free collection of stickers printed with my name and address, presumably to be affixed to my outgoing mail. I really appreciated getting those stickers as I think they are convenient to own.

But the letter was from the Alzheimer's Association and the first line read as follows: "grandma doesn't know me anymore" I was absolutely devastated!

Did they send the stickers because they didn't think I remember where I live?

Had they also contacted my grandchildren? And did those grandchildren really think I don't know them any longer? Which ones were they anyway? I have so many and sometimes I can't remember their names. I believe there are 9 or maybe 10 or even 11. They really seem to multiply.

I certainly know where I live, especially in Florida where I'm spending the winter—My New York address is hard to recall. But anyway I won't be there for awhile—I think I'm returning in April or maybe May. No doubt someone will let me know when I'm going back.

I know that Alzheimer's is what older people get, so why did those people write to me? Or did they call me? At any rate I know I'm perfectly fine. At least I was yesterday or certainly last week.

I definitely know a lot of people by name, but some others look so different that I can't quite place them.

Sometimes people greet me and I don't think I ever knew them. Maybe they want to sell me something. You have to be really careful these days. Also when I see these people they occasionally ask me "don't you know my name"? Isn't that ridiculous. If they don't know their name why should I?

Anyway if you can explain what that letter meant I would appreciate your calling me. But I just can't remember my telephone number right now, so write to me instead—You'll find my address on one of those stickers.

OLD FRIENDS

On a recent Sunday morning I made a list of seven old friends whom I had neglected of late and decided to call them. I was looking forward to casual chatting and hoping to catch up on their family escapades, as well as their own daily doings.

The first person I called said she was feeling very depressed due to a back injury, her husband's demise, the large house in Florida that she was unable to sell due to the market turndown, and the absence of social activities she was used to enjoying. Needless to say, I was saddened to hear her woeful tale.

The next person said she had recently fallen, broken three ribs and was in a very painful state.

The third person explained that her diagnosis of dementia was resulting in her feeling very "crotchety" and unable to perform many easy tasks. She also could not remember where I lived.

The fourth person, who was usually jovial and energetic told me a lung biopsy she had a few days ago was not benign.

By this time I decided I would not call the other three on my list. I'm now going to e-mail everyone with just a cheery message.

WHY ARE "WE" DOING THIS

Why are we doing this? I say *"we"* which is actually an editorial *"we"* because it is really *"me"* who is doing this and what the "me" is doing is having 30 people for thanksgiving dinner.

30 people—Wow! I must have been utterly out of my mind when I called these people individually, and ever so graciously extended my invitation and horrors! They all accepted. Of course they all seem to be healthy, attractive, personable, and had their flu shots. But apparently no other invitations had been extended to any of them, so they all accepted mine.

Besides, who else would be foolish enough to entertain the *idea* of inviting 30 people to dinner in an apartment. In fact, I'd rather entertain the *idea* than entertain all of *them*—oh well, I guess I'd better plan my menu. So here goes.

Hors D'oeuves, such as fresh shrimp and a vegetable dip platter will be a necessity, because that will keep all my guests out of the kitchen, and they will hopefully munch and chew for at least a half hour, which will allow me time to baste my very large turkey, unmold my absolutely fantastic cranberry, orange, walnut connection, which I will decorate with navel orange slices and watercress.

Then I can keep an eye on my stuffing casserole (which I must confess is the very best) consisting of fresh chestnuts, celery, onions, carrots, bread cubes, mushrooms, turkey giblets, parsley, sage, chicken soup and butter, and which will be presented in a large Pyrex bowl encased in a silver container.

Creamed white baby onions are always nice, and with a little paprika on top, will look great. Also brussel sprouts with a bread crumb dressing always adds a little color to the table.

For dessert, I guess I'll need several enticing items.

A pumpkin chiffon pie with whipped cream on top, lace cookies, and of course homemade strawberry shortcake with a bountiful display of berries will prove to be the "pièce de resistance".

Naturally, I'll keep the wine glasses well filled so that my guests will be so soused that they'll all want to go home early, giving me time to do the dishes and generally clean up within a reasonable amount of time.

I'm positive everybody will thank me profusely, and I will vocally minimize the efforts I put forth for this dinner and probably invite them all back for next year's holiday—same time, same place.

Then after they leave and I finish cleaning and straightening up, I can finally go to bed and have my heart attack in peace!

I'M NEVER GOING TO DO ANYTHING I DON'T WANT TO DO EVER AGAIN!

All of my life I was such a good person. As a young child I would never do anything that was considered to be wrong.

If my parents said: do thus and so", I practically ran to obey.

As I got older this behavior continued. I did everything my companions suggested. If they wanted to go to the movies, I acquiesced, if they wanted to go to the beach, I dashed home to get a bathing suit. If they wished to go to a restaurant known to have terrible food, I was the first one to rave about the dinner.

I never smoked, drank, or even got a driving ticket. Laws were made for me, just so I could obey them.

I was particularly vigilant about being on time for appointments. I was so nice it was disgusting.

Now however, I have aged, and with my increasing years, I've developed a wonderful confidence that allows me the freedom to be myself and do exactly what I wish to do.

Now I won't eat anything I don't like, I won't go to a place not of my liking, and I don't care what anyone thinks.

I would expound at great length on my changing ways in this regard, but I have an appointment and I don't want to be late!

THEY GIVE—I TAKE

I have a confession to make—I'm guilty of purchasing an inordinate number of cosmetics in "give away programs" which generally include free colognes, lipsticks, day creams, night creams, mascaras, as well as make-up bags, handbags, travel bags and even items useful for "under the eye bags".

I diligently peruse the "Sunday Times" every week to find out which company is giving away the most intriguing items, and duly purchase the cosmetics with the greatest number of "I can't resist" gifts.

So at the present I own almost 500 lipsticks, 400 mascara sticks, 300 travel bags and 400 tubes of various creams.

Occasionally I use one or two of these preparations. The rest are arrayed nicely in a special set of cabinets I have in my bathroom.

They really look great on these cabinet shelves and every so often I give them a second glance. Sometimes I'm even tempted to use the travel bags, which are usually very colorful and attractive. But then I realize my old ones are still good so why should I use the new ones.

As for the lipsticks, they are most likely the wrong color for me, and I guess that's why they are "giveaways"—nobody likes the color they give away.

In addition I don't have much faith in the day or night creams so I don't use them at all, which is probably why I still have wrinkles.

Nevertheless the delightful idea of getting all these supposedly free items for a nominal sum, is so exciting that I can't resist the temptation to send for them.

I sincerely hope that someday soon these cosmetic companies will stop giving all these things away so I can refrain from buying them, and be able to save enough money to have cosmetic surgery,

"TIME WILL TELL"

I am always early. Actually I'm a truly compulsive "on time" or "early person", consequently I'm used to waiting for other people to show up for lunch, bridge, theatre, etc.

If I'm invited to a party and arrive by car, I am compelled to keep driving around the block so I'm not the first guest to arrive.

However, since turning our clocks forward for daylight savings time, I have a big problem; "spring forward" is to blame.

I miss that extra hour of sleep and therefore I've become a "late person". I have already missed an important doctor's appointment and since my MD is now on a month's vacation, I found it necessary to call a new "curing" guy.

Also, I've peeved three bridge friends, as I've been very late for several games, leaving them as a threesome.

Then too, my beauty Parlor knows it can't rely on my promptness any longer and I probably will have to take canasta lessons, as my bridge friends have divorced me.

It's a given that I'm no longer welcome at my beauty shop, even though they know I'm contrite.

So now, I can't wait until November to get my hour back.

A MEDICAL MEMORY

I have a particular medical memory which is not easily forgotten.

Two years ago I went to a new gynecologist for my yearly check-up.

This gentleman, whom I had never met, had recently taken over the practice from the estate of my former Gyn who had unfortunately passed away.

After a short wait, I was ushered into an examining room, instructed to remove most of my clothing, and to lie down on the table in the standard position (i.e legs in the stirrups) for the exam. Naturally a nurse was in attendance.

The doctor arrived, briefly introduced himself and then adjusted the lamp he was holding so that he could peer into me and pass judgment on his findings.

He then addressed the nurse in this manner—quote "this one is dying—in fact, the one that was in here yesterday died too" unquote.

Naturally I was most upset after hearing these disturbing words, and in a tremulous tone of voice asked if he was referring to me.

Oh no he said quote "I was talking about my lamp—it's broken" unquote.

All three of us got hysterical laughing and after that we were able to establish a very nice relationship and besides I got a good report.

GETTING LOST

I have finally reached the age whereby many of my acquaintances, and in some instances really good friends have begun to "lose it a bit" as they say.

I know this is probably inevitable in the aging process, but it certainly is disconcerting, as the following incident will explain.

Recently I received two invitations to the same luncheon from 2 different people. I accepted the first one to arrive and when I declined the second, my would be hostess didn't quite understand that I was unable to be her guest.

She called me 5 or 6 times during the ensuing weeks saying she was looking forward to me being her guest, and to seeing me.

I tried very hard to explain that I would *indeed* be seeing her there, but not as her guest. Each time she said she understood, but then would call again the following week with the same message. These back and forth calls continued until the day of the luncheon.

That day finally arrived and I was sitting next to my official hostess, when my other friend arrived and warmly embraced my hostess. She mentioned how happy she was to see *her* and never acknowledged me. She honestly did not recognize me! I was fearful that the same thing could happen to me. So when my daughter called the next day, I asked her to please tell me who *she* is.

DISASTER IN THE CLOSET

An unfortunate incident has taken place in my life lately, and I am at a complete loss as to how I can rectify the situation.

I seem to have become a victim of a series of break-ins in my apartment.

Items have really not been stolen; however, they have been thoroughly transformed. Apparently, some evil person enters my home without my knowledge, gets into my closets, and performs extremely dastardly deeds.

He or she, with a total disregard for my feelings, takes every item of my clothing and deliberately sews them into smaller sizes.

Therefore, I can no longer fit into any jacket, dress, sweater, etc. They are all now much too tight.

Since I am out of the house a great deal, it is impossible to catch these people at their sly machinations and why they would even perform such nasty activities is beyond me.

I've already changed my door locks and have bought new keys, but somehow they still manage to enter my home.

As I have nothing to wear any longer, the situation is becoming disastrous.

A sad affect of this problem is that I have taken to nonstop eating. This is a nervous reaction no doubt.

If I don't catch these wicked folks soon, I guess I'll have to move, or maybe go on a diet..

SERVICE WITH A SMILE?

The other day my washing machine broke down, and after calling the manufacturer for repair service, I was told in a recording that someone would get back to me.

I waited patiently to no avail, and after 15 minutes of holding on, I hung up and tried their alternative number.

This time I was told in another recording that my waiting time would be 20 minutes. I was rewarded with a loud and very unpleasant musical rendition of an awful song.

My 20 minutes were finally up and my ears were both hurting terribly, even though I kept shifting the phone from one ear to the other, but there was still no response.

In desperation, I called a local store that carried my brand of washing machine and was given a new number for repairs and this time a real person answered.

I was so happy, but just to be sure he was genuine, I asked him to verify it and the answer was a definite yes.

However, his accent was so thick, I could hardly understand him, nor could he seem to understand me.

I then asked "where are you calling from". In a very polite tone he responded "India" then when I asked if he could send someone to fix my broken washing machine; he replied "alas—an airplane ticket would be too expensive".

I thoroughly agreed with him, so now I use a local laundry service.

A MOVING EXPERIENCE

Recently I experienced a complete upheaval in my wonderful way of life. I walked around my rather large apartment and realized that a thorough paint job was in order.

Walls would have to be scrapped, sanded and possibly "3 paint coated" to bring them back to a pristine state.

This of course would entail emptying clothes closets, dish cabinets, recovering and polishing furniture and a probable discarding of unwanted and no longer usable objects. In fact at least 2 months of disarray was ahead of me.

I was already lamenting this and decided I would have to move to a hotel during the painting process.

However being absolutely brilliant (a moot point), I listened to the light bulb that went off in my head and decided to buy an already redecorated apartment in what is known as mint condition, and which was happily available in my current building complex. I would only be moving from one building to another and figured it would be a snap.

Every morning for 2 weeks, starting at 7AM, so that I would not disturb my neighbors, I pushed grocery carts loaded with dishes, bric-a-brac, linens, books and paintings to my new apartment. This took 2 to 3 hours daily pushing back and forth after which I would collapse for a few hours and then continue the routine for another 2 hours.

Later in the afternoon I leisurely (with some friendly help) put my belongings into their respective new spots.

My clothes were lined up color coordinated on their closet poles, dishes, probably never to be used, were ensconced in the kitchen cupboards, books were placed on the already existing book shelves, linens rewashed and neatly folded were placed in their new closet, and there I was all ready for the movers to bring in the furniture I was keeping. The things to be recovered were at the upholsterers who promised a prompt delivery. It was a breeze! I was so smart to do this.

Finally the official moving day arrived and my furniture was put in place without mishap—great—now I was able to enjoy a leisurely dinner in the coffee shop in my building and read the newspaper in my new digs.

First however I thought I had better call my daughter in Florida to let her know I was now in my new apartment.

Unfortunately the telephone did not work. It seems there was no outlet in the bedroom. The previous owner had cut the outlet wires as they only used hand held phones from another room. I was used to land phones and apparently could not have service in the bedroom unless I bought a hand held phone.

Then I thought I would turn on the TV which was supposedly an existing top of the line unit encased in the wall. It had DVD, HDTV, etc. Alas it did not have a cable connection. The heck with it, I thought, I'll just go to bed—after all it was a really full day.

So I tried to plug my night light in the bathroom. No dice!

The plug went the opposite way on the wall and I could not put in my night light because there was no room on the wall to reverse it—nevertheless I wearily got into bed.

4:30AM I awakened and decided to go to the bathroom but couldn't find it in the dark (my lamp unfortunately was on the other side of the bed) and tho I remembered where my former bathroom was, this one was not in the same place.

It was then that I realized I was a stranger in my own home

LADIES NIGHT OUT

On a recent late Saturday afternoon I was accompanied by 6 other ladies and we all attended a motion picture at the complex in which we live.

After the film was over we decided to have a light bite at the restaurant which is also on the premises.

There we were—a very noisy group arriving en masse in an already crowded dining place.

Luckily we found a sizeable round table, and the group practically played musical chairs in deciding who should sit where.

Finally we all settled in and the patient waiter tried to figure out who wanted what.

One lady ordered a tongue sandwich which had to be "middle cuts, no end cuts, no little pieces and not as bad as the one I had last week".

Another one couldn't decide what to order, until someone else placed *her* order and then the first lady said she wanted the same thing.

Still another one wanted a hamburger, but it had to be just right, not too well done, not too rare, not too thick and not too thin.

I must admit I was just as finicky. I wanted pea soup—not too thick, preferably diluted with chicken soup and very hot.

The remaining ladies were just as decisive as to their orders and the understanding waiter finally scratched his head in confusion and left—hopefully to return with the proper items and in the appropriate manner.

A lively conversation then ensued with each lady offering an amusing remark.

It was finally decided that I should write an article about this evening's activities, and so I took out my writing pad and proceeded to take notes.

Words started flying out of each person's mouth, one wanted to be sure I'd spell her name right, another one wanted to know if I'd pay them for the information I'd receive—still another one thought we should all reveal "dirt" about our former lives. Of course all of those other innocent ladies demurred violently when that suggestion was made.

We then heard about the very handsome young man who was so popular in the high school another lady had attended and whom she never forgot. After that some lady mentioned that her son made the most wonderful mushroom and barley soup in his luxury take out shop. (I'm supposed to get some) and sadly we heard that another lady had her scarf stolen by some evil person at a recent function held at our complex.

Differing opinions were offered as to the supposed purloining of that scarf and ultimately it was decided that maybe the scarf really belonged to the person who took it, because it matched her outfit.

The most vehement turn in the conversation concerned a problem 3 of the ladies were having in a Bridge game—they were all unhappy with a 4th player and tried to devise methods in which they could get rid of her.

This situation could not be resolved in a satisfactory manner so apparently the lady in question will remain as a player in that game.

Much hilarity and discourse continued to flow, and generally speaking it was a fun evening spent with lovely ladies.

I courageously left first so I'm not sure what they said about me, and my eccentricities, which include my retiring and rising at unusually early hours.

But it doesn't really matter what they say about me, as, *I'm able to get even with this article.*

MY LOVELY GREAT GRANDCHILDREN?

I always thought it would be wonderful to finally become a great grandmother, but it can also have its disadvantages.

As an example—I recently spent a few days in Chicago visiting a granddaughter who had moved there a few months ago. She has 2 beautiful, bright and lovely children, and I was very anxious to spend time with them.

However, in the early part of my visit, Jordan, who is 11 years old, inquired as to why I do not have white hair. Before I was able to make up a plausible excuse, Lauren, who is 8 ½ piped up "Jordan what's the matter with you—don't you know? She dyes it". Of course I was slightly mortified and hoped my roots were not showing, nevertheless the incident was forgotten.

Shortly afterwards these two children innocently asked me if I would like to play a card game with them. I amiably said yes, thinking, as most great grandparents would, that I'd have to pretend to be a loser so that these youngsters could enjoy being winners.

The card game we played was unknown to me. It's called "phase ten" and consists of a special deck containing several wild cards, and also another group of cards, which a player who has one, can announce that another particular person would lose his playing turn the next time around. The object of the game is to finally have very few or no points left, and to complete 10 different groups of cards arranged in a designated order

I was all set to play and my little opponents were ready also.

Somehow I became their victim. Those 2 completely outfoxed me. They got all the wild cards, and if I had a good hand they conspired to use their special rule preventing me to have my turn.

I tried my best to outwit them to no avail. I yelled—"you cheat! You're both evil". This outburst didn't sway them one bit. They *stood* or should I say *sat* their ground!

I continued to vehemently whine but wound up losing 550 points to their winning scores, and those two little devils simply smirked gleefully.

To make matters worse, Lauren said "tough—big grandma". "This is how we're supposed to play the game"!

As I stated before, I had magnanimously and willingly intended to lose to them, but I did not expect to lose legitimately—what a defeat and certainly most embarrassing. They also told me that no one had ever lost that many points. I had set a record!

We finally left Chicago so I didn't have to play the game with them again. However they are coming to Florida this Christmas and they are bringing the cards with them and invited me to play again—Oh God—help me!

HOW OLD IS OLD?

This morning I got up very early and felt particularly spry and young. I started to straighten out my closets, then my dresser drawers and pretty soon it was time for lunch and I was a bit weary.

After lunch I went through my desk drawers, then my linen closet and started to tackle my refrigerator as well but suddenly felt a bit older than I had in the morning so I stopped for a little nap.

A nice cup of afternoon tea was refreshing and then I decided to clean my medicine cabinet. Immediately afterwards I felt *very* much older and absolutely exhausted.

I had to skip dinner, pop into bed at 8 PM and figured out that I had probably advanced in age at least 10 years all in one day.

I then realized getting older is not easy and I hired a housekeeper!

THE UPS AND DOWNS OF LIFE

I have a problem—I live in an apartment building on the 23rd floor and sometimes want to go *down* to the lower level. So what button do I push? If I push *down* the elevator has to come *up* first, so don't I have to push *up*? But if I push *up*—how does the elevator know I want to go *down*? Sometimes I push *up* and the elevator goes right up to the penthouse—so it definitely didn't know I wanted it to come *up* so I could go *down*—on the other hand when I push *down,* it sometimes comes *up* and if I get inside, it keeps going *up* anyway—this is so troublesome that I think I have to stay home.

THE WONDERFUL YEARS

During the past several years a number of my contemporaries departed from this world; and since then I've noticed that the attitude of the less aged people than myself have considerably changed towards me.

As for instance, at a recent luncheon I attended, there were many guests who were quite young and whom I had not seen for quite a while.

Surprisingly, at least 8 or 9 of them approached me with these words "you look wonderful, really you do, what is your secret? Naturally these comments were very complimentary. However, when I thought about them that evening, I came to the conclusion that these people didn't actually mean that I look wonderful.

What they really meant was "my god, I didn't think you were still alive".

REALLY RICH

I can't believe it, I'm very rich. I saved so much money recently, and I'm not even through counting it.

First of all I did not buy a new car, even though my present car is several years old. This certainly saved me about $60,000.

Then that old sofa bed in my den became disreputable, so I purchased a blow up bed instead—a savings of $3000.

There was a wonderful fur sale at Saks and I could possibly have bought a lovely mink coat, instead I took a discount night flight to Florida for the winter (where I definitely do not need furs) thereby saving about $3500.

Also, I wanted a new pair of black dress shoes and the sale at Ferragamos sounded great, but then I took my old ones to the shoemaker, who put new tips and heels on them, and they were to have a nice shine as well. That saved me at least $300

Then I walked to my daughter's house at the North end of town, a gas saving of $1.50.

I only ate 2 meals a day for 2 weeks which saved about $175.00.

Going to bed early for a few weeks helped me save on electricity and TV costs. (I didn't get my bills yet so I'm not sure how much was the savings).

I'm really quite satisfied with all these savings except that I had to go to a few doctors yesterday, as well as a repair person.

You see I developed a bad blister on my foot while walking to my daughter's house, I had a stomach ache from not eating properly. My old car broke down completely, and I'm having 2 guests sleeping at my house and the blow up bed leaks and therefore won't blow up, so now I have to put them up at a hotel.

I also had to go to the eye doctor, because I strained my eyes from reading in my bed in the dark, and the shoemaker lost my shoes.

I'm now thinking of going back to New York for the rest of the winter and have to pay the full airline price. The worst thing of all, I don't have a warm coat!

The good thing though is that I saved a lot of money.

THINGS LEFT UNDONE

If I made a list of all the things I've left undone in my life there would not be enough paper to contain the words.

Sure—I could list left over laundry to be done, a visit to the drugstore to buy toothpaste, or newspapers to be perused, since these were probably piled up at least 20 inches after a week of not being read.

Perhaps even unpaid bills, unreturned phone calls, thank you, or condolences notes to be written and numerous other mundane items.

But most of all I should list letters of appreciation and thank you's to all those who've made my life so worthwhile, and to god who has given me good health, and especially to my wonderful family, my numerous dear *old* friends and gratefully for my *new* friends.

My list is truly never ending.

LEARNING TO DRIVE

Palm Beach Florida is a very versatile community. It has lovely weather for the most part (if you don't mind daily rainstorms) and you can closely associate with people from many other states, plus being able to visit all of the shops that display beautiful clothes (which may or not be affordable!)

Also expensive and colorful foreign cars are the norm, and most people have walkers, either the mechanical variety or in some cases the social types.

"The Shiney Sheet" helps you hobnob with the elite in an objective sense, and in general the town is a winter paradise.

However Palm Beach also has another side. It is very close to West Palm Beach which is totally different. I can attest to that and I will explain how I can prove it.

In the late 1940's when Palm Beach was my winter home, I found it necessary to learn how to drive. We had just acquired a new car, which was unusual, as it was just after the 2nd World War and automobiles were at a premium.

But since my brother-in-law was a Buick dealer in Peoria, Illinois we were fortunately able to buy a brand new very big, very blue Buick. However, I could not drive it.

At that time my husband was in the jewelry business in P.B. and had a retired police officer guarding his establishment. His name was Jerry Connelly and he kindly offered to give me driving lessons. What could be better—I might never get a ticket!

Jerry and I spent many days on North County Road, which at the time was practically empty and we also found a circular roadway near MiraFlores Drive, where I lived, and where I could go round and round to my heart's content.

In any event, Jerry soon pronounced me ready for my test, which would take place in West Palm. However I did not know how to park one car behind the other because in Palm Beach in those days they only had diagonal parking, which made parallel parking unnecessary. You see everything here was geared to ease the lives of Palm Beachers.

Sadly I then found out that in West Palm the test required the proper parking ability, and I was naturally quite nervous. But not to worry! Because Jerry was entirely confident that I would pass and I soon learned how he knew.

He said all I had to do was place a Shiny, new $5.00 bill on the seat space between me and the tester and I would automatically get my license—which I did!!

I am sure you now realize why I am so enthralled with Palm Beach. We really take care of our own.

IF I COULD DO IT OVER AGAIN

A long time ago, while living in Palm Beach as an ordinary mother, wife and winter resident, I was suddenly asked to participate in an exciting experience.

Some friends from Illinois arrived in a private plane enroute to Nassau for the weekend.

They very kindly invited me to fly with them to Nassau just for lunch, which was certainly an intriguing idea.—

Little did I know that the plane was a small Beechcraft only able to carry 4 people, a pilot, my 2 friends and me. Also to get on the plane we were all required to wear safety jackets and had to board by climbing on the wing in order to gain entry to the plane.

In my real life I was hardly able to ride an escalator.—

However I did indeed fly to Nassau and had a wonderful lunch, wandered about, made a few lovely purchases and then re-entered the plane for my return trip. My friends of course were remaining in Nassau.

The pilot invited me to sit up front with him which I considered to be a very friendly gesture.—

But halfway home and over the water he said "why don't you fly the plane now". I looked around and since there was no one else on board I realized he meant me!

Oh God! I thought but took the joy stick in my shaking hand and then did what he said I should.

For half an hour I pushed the stick up and down, and right and left as I was instructed and when looking ahead over the water and with just the beautiful sky above—I felt the closest to being religious and to God as was possible. I never was so exhilarated in my entire life and couldn't wait to get home to tell my family about my great adventure.

And if I could do it over again, I would!

BRRR!!!!

I'm cold, I'm really cold! Actually freezing! Maybe Frozen!

I live in Florida where my heating apparatus isn't working. I took a cold shower this A.M. and now I'm sitting in a chair, I'm wrapped in a cashmere throw, and completely encased in a snuggie, but my extremities are all stiff and cold, even my nose is red and cold.

This is a really terrible situation. I believe it is 32 degrees outside and think it must be the same inside, especially in this supposedly luxury apartment.

I keep drinking hot tea and then I have to go to the bathroom and the toilet seat is cold,—I wish I was a boy!

What to do? I live facing the intercoastal where the water is presently bouncing all around and it even appears to have snow caps on it.

I must say this is not the vacation land I was looking forward to enjoying.

I think I would be better off in Alaska, Maybe Sarah Palin has room for me. I hear she is pretty "hot stuff".

MONDAY 8 AM THIS MORNING THE SKY FELL DOWN IN FLORIDA

The most terrible thing has happened. This morning the sky fell down right onto the intercoastal waterway, which my apartment faces, and now West Palm Beach is completely gone. I can't see any signs of it.

Calamity of Calamities. How can I get to Costco? I'll have to buy my books full price and what about Bed Bath and Beyond. No more gadgets, and my favorite restaurant, that good pasta at La Sirena, Oh god! I had tickets to Kravis too!

How could this happen?—Supposing I get sick? All my doctors are in West Palm Beach, and what about Good Sam, supposing I need a hospital. Thank goodness my Dentist is in Palm Beach proper, but anyway I just had my teeth cleaned.

What about the airport? How can I go home? I'll be stuck in Palm Beach for the hot summer. Nobody in their right minds would want that.

I definitely remember the story of Chicken Little. He predicted that the sky would fall, so maybe he had a link to Nostradamus. I read that book but don't remember any verse on fallen skies.

Who can I call? I don't think god has a cell phone and besides, I don't have his number, and why would he help me anyway, I'm not that religious.

Even the movies are in West Palm and I never got to see the Oscar contenders. I certainly don't need clothes, so Worth Avenue is out. What to do? Maybe I'll go to temple and pray.

P.S. This is Tuesday, the next day at 9AM, the heavy fog is gone, the sun is shining brightly, and lo and behold West Palm is back, so finally all's right with my world.

P.P.S. I'm glad I prayed!

ATTENTION! LAUNDRY ROOM—
333 SUNSET AVE, PALM BEACH, FLA

To whom it may concern! Sad to say, on a recent laundry day one of my dearest possessions disappeared.

This article was very close to my heart and especially to my bosom. It was a brand new white lacey bra.

Unfortunately since this occurrence took place, my spirits have been very crest fallen, and my bosom too has fallen from its crest.

The loss of this bra has been a "downer" in more ways than one.

I sincerely hope all you washer ladies will keep abreast of this situation and see that the aforementioned bra will be returned to me, it's rightful owner.

Its return will be an uplift to my spirits and indeed to other parts of my anatomy.

A suitable reward is offered and then my "cups will runneth over with joy"

Thank you
Bernice Zakin

TURN LEFT OR TURN RIGHT

Sometime ago while I was in Florida, I made arrangements to visit an old friend, or should I say "one of long standing".

At any rate we were planning to have a Bridge game at her home, and I was there with another friend, who was driving us in her car.

Now I have a confession to make—I have a renowned reputation for not knowing east from west, nor north from south, except at the Bridge table.

People always tell me that the east in Florida is near the ocean, and so I ask them "how do I know where the ocean is if I am inland? Then they tell me the west is where the sun sets, but again I ask "supposing it's a cloudy day and there is no visible sunshine? I always receive the same reply—no answer! Thus I have never figured out how these people are so smart about directions.

Nevertheless this day I was trying to give my driving friend the proper instructions as to how we could get to our Bridge hostess, and kept glancing at the directions she (the hostess) had given me (which incidentally were incorrect).

Where it said turn left at Donald Ross, we tried to do so, but landed at a dead end, and after a 10 minute turn around, we then continued to where we were supposed to arrive at US 1.

But I didn't know if US 1 was the same as A1A alternate, nor did my driver know this, so after another 15 minutes, we finally arrived at the real US1, but definitely could not find the proper turnoff.

I then called 411 to get the telephone number of our Bridge hostess's apartment complex and happily discovered that we were just one block away.

The good news concerning this adventure was that we had worried about arriving too early, and thank heavens we arrived fashionably late!

TIME SPENT ALONE IN PALM BEACH, FLA

Alone at last—this is really exciting—what a luxury-nothing to do. I can actually sleep late maybe until 9 A.M. and not feel guilty.

I don't even have to get dressed—I can just lounge in a robe. The NY times can lie there for all I care—I don't have to read about Tiger, Iraq, Schwartzenager, the Giants, or the after Christmas Sales—nothing except maybe the obituary notices—I can't ignore those—I might miss a funeral.

There is positively no one around to disturb my trend of thoughts—no one to demand anything from me—even the telephone can become a nonentity if I don't pick up. Thank Heavens for voice mail in case of emergencies.

I can gaze out the window and watch the boats sail along the intercoastal, or maybe dance around the room to a merry tune on the radio—the choices are myriad and all mine. I can even have a half sour pickle or a tootsie roll and it's only 10:30 AM wow! What a happy thought!

Also, I can just sit "perchance to dream" as Shakespeare said and maybe I'll even read some Shakespeare.

All I know is that this is truly the good life so why do most other people feel compelled to fill their days with accomplishments—this dawdling is much more to my liking.

Furthermore, I can reread letters from dead friends, there are certainly loads of those (both friends and letters) or look at old photo albums, tho I probably won't recognize most of the people.

And I can even make lists—I love lists! I can write really long ones and not ever do anything on them—it's a great activity.

This kind of day is precious and rare, and if someone calls tomorrow and asks what I did yesterday, all I have to do is say "nothing special".

THE HAMPTONS

The Hamptons in the Spring are very lovely
And also are the Hamptons in the Fall
But when summertime arrives
And despite the lengthy drives
The Hamptons are a pleasure for us all

If you lie upon the beach and watch the ocean
And listen to the rhythm of the waves
It's like a fairy land
Albeit in the sand
And everyone who does it raves and raves

Antiquing too's a fun thing to be doing
It's a very pleasing form of recreation
You can almost always find
A "thing" one of a kind
A reminder when back home of your vacation

Plus restaurants and food stores are abundant
Especially with lobsters and with clams
At Citarella and at Tates
You don't mind the endless waits
As long as you can buy their fish and yummy jams

And the shopping too is so enticing
Plus everything displayed is just so nice
So for every gal and guy
The great things you can buy
Will make you soon forget the hefty price

Then even if you're only summer renting
And have to face the fact each season ends
Your income may go higher
And you might become a buyer
So *next year* you can *come back*
And make new friends

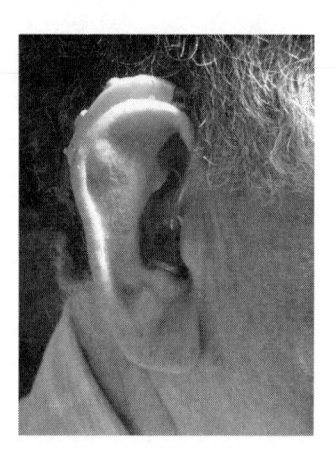

HEARING

You know what really bugs me? Young people today mumble their words so badly that it is impossible to hear or understand a word they say.

I don't care what wonderful schools they attended, they certainly never learned diction. As for instance, my children as well as my grandchildren are guilty of the worst speech patterns possible.

I can be sitting in a room or a restaurant with them and I have to keep asking, what did you say or what did he say—it is just awful.

Also I now find that a lot of my friends have the same habit. Most of them don't speak well either.

Even the telephone people who call for donations are just as bad. How can I figure out where to send my charity checks if I can't hear them. On the other hand, most of these people are from other countries so maybe that's the problem.

Anyway, this is getting to be a very annoying situation and if it continues, I may have to get a hearing aid.

THE HOUSE GUESTS

Oh God! Why did I invite them—I really thought it was for just three days—who knew we'd have a tornado warning, and now they have to stay!

I absolutely don't understand these people—they never offer to do anything helpful, and they are disgustingly sloppy about themselves. When I am a house guest I'm so careful to be tidy, almost to an extreme—but they on the contrary leave cigarette butts all over—ashes on the tables and floor, cracker crumbs wherever they sit and I don't think they ever thought about putting on shoes. If I see one more naked toe, I think I'll scream!

The worst thing is that they want me to change the position of my sofa so that they will be able to get the early morning sun. Don't they realize fabrics can fade?

Well thank heavens they are leaving this afternoon. In fact I'm confirming their flight time now.

Oh please! Somebody help me! Their flight's been cancelled!

25 THINGS I HATE

1. A new toilet paper roll that wont unroll without my tearing it.

2. Pill containers that won't turn to the right place in order to open easily.

3. Telephones that stop ringing just as I run to pick up the receiver—and then no one answers.

4. Jelly and butter pats that are hard to open in coffee shops.

5. Trying to pick up dropped soap in the far end of the shower while holding onto the rod.

6. Water that suddenly turns cold while I'm in the shower.

7. When my nail breaks off at the nail bed.

8. When my nail polish smears just after a manicure.

9. Trying to hook a bra that is slightly too small.

10. A stopped up toilet during the night.

11. Spattering pasta tomato sauce on a new white blouse.

12. Carrying an umbrella in a torrential rain—and it won't open.

13. Constantly getting only 3or 4 high card points in a bridge hand.

14. Not being able to find my house or car keys.

15. Having curly hair on a humid day.

16. Waiting home all day for an appliance repair man who doesn't show up.

17. Not being able to remember somebody's name.

18. Having a bus driver close the door just before I try to get on.

19. Having the elevator close the door just before I try to enter.

20. Tough steak and cold soup.

21. Trying to fasten a necklace in the back when I'm going out and I'm a little late.

22. Trying to *un*fasten a necklace in the back when I'm coming home and I'm tired.

23. Opening a spice container incorrectly and having half of it spill into my food.

24. Dropping a good dish and having it shatter all over the kitchen floor.

25. Going on a trip and forgetting to pack a necessary item.

SHOULD WE EAT PIZZA STANDING UP

And should meatballs and Borscht be on the same dinner menu?

Some people might think the title of this little tale is unusual and peculiar. Not so—a great deal of aforethought has gone into the reasoning behind the selection of these words.

Now—as for the pizza—Everyone knows that the person actually making pizza does so in a standing position. Sometimes the dough itself is gracefully tossed into the air—occasionally flipped in a fanciful way with a high arc, and at other times in a more mundane fashion, lower in height.

After that all the colorful and enticing aromatic veggies are artfully arranged on the now carefully patted down dough, all the while with the pizza chef grounded on his heels and wishing he could be sitting. This poor guy is obligated to either stand in a windowed area in a so called pizza parlor, or behind the counter near a scorching hot brick pizza oven—no wonder he usually has unhealthy appearing red cheeks and very stiff legs. No wonder too that he might prefer having a different occupation.

Now to the nitty gritty—should the average pizza eater sit or stand while feasting upon this delicious tidbit?

My non professional opinion would be to stand—out of deference to the preparers need to do so, but also because *it* (the pizza slice) is usually eaten without the need for cutlery, therefore there is actually no need to sit.

Meatballs and Borscht is an autre chose entirely. This combination did not originate with me. It actually was mentioned by my son, when, as an interested mother I inquired as to what was his favorite food combination.

I thoroughly understood the meatballs, as Kenny my son spent his junior year of college in Florence Italy, and has been a very efficient Italian cook ever since that period of his life, so he really loved meatballs.

But Borscht!—wherever did he come up with that idea. First of all my husband hated beets, and they never appeared in our household. I myself never tasted Borscht, and to me even the coloration of that combination is unpleasant. Brown meatballs and bubble gum pink Borscht are not arte nouveau, not Victorian, not regency and not at all pleasant

Taste wise the combo in my opinion would not be palatable if they were ever served together, and I don't think it would appeal to the average gourmet officianado—a gourmand—maybe.

So all in all I think I have to negate the combination.

Therefore if any of you are ever invited to my home for dinner do not expect to find these items among the offerings—In fact—do not expect an invitation at all—as I no longer cook.

MY SON

I have a very sad story to tell. I believe I am a failure as a mother, as I am having great difficulties with my son, relating to a particular situation.

Mind you, my son was a wonderful little boy, a lovely young man, presently a fine member of his community, as well as a good husband and father. But of late, he's thoroughly impossible!

As for instance, he has been calling me very often with an ongoing complaint. His feet hurt, his shoes don't fit properly and he has to put ice on his toes every evening to relieve the pain.

When I inquire as to how this condition occurred, I get the same answer. It seems that the many pairs of Gucci shoes he has been buying and wearing for 25 years no longer are comfortable. He claims that Gucci doesn't make them the same way they did previously, and that the nice little Italian man who formerly made them either died or moved to China, where they are now manufactured.

He also lamented that he has to wear old sneakers to business, and replace them with his ill fitting shoes while at work. This of course is both painful and embarrassing.

When I asked when he last had his feet measured, he was insulted. "Why would I do that", he peevishly inquired?

I patiently replied that as one grows older, every part of the body is subject to change, including the feet. I also suggested that he have his shoes stretched, his feet measured, and that he possibly purchase the next size shoe when buying a new pair.

This advice seemed incomprehensible to him, and he continued to blame the Chinese and expressed the intention to sue them. As he is an attorney, this seemed quite logical to him because then the lawsuit proceedings would be free.

In desperation, I've had to discontinue answering my telephone at 9:30 PM, which is when he generally calls me, so as to avoid these sore feet conversations!

His wife, I might add, usually goes to the movies on these evenings and I don't blame her.

I KNOW IT'S NOT IMPORTANT BUT IT KEEPS EATING AT ME!

I'm pleased to say I love my daughter Nancy dearly. She is really the best, and I am truly fortunate to be her mother.

However, even though I realize it's of no consequence, she does something that absolutely drives me crazy and in addition it causes me to lose a lot of sleep.

This is the situation—Nancy has a Blackberry. Not only does she have one—it positively *owns* her.

Her thumbs are constantly engaged in manipulating the little letters and numbers, and of course she is glued to the screen.

If we are in a restaurant together day or night, I really never see her face. I only see the tops of her hands.

If we are in a car or taxi her thumbs are continually moving.

If I ask her a question, she usually answers the person on the Blackberry before speaking to me, and certainly never looks at me.

But that is not the worst—are you ready?

Nancy and her husband Jeff very often go on trips where the time difference may be several hours. In that case if she is in a restaurant in Paris eating fabulous food, I am probably sound asleep in America, maybe even enjoying a pleasant dream.

Then all of a sudden my phone rings and when I groggily answer, all I hear is Nancy busily engaged in a conversation, either with friends, the waiter or her husband.

They keep chatting away—I keep shouting and of course they don't hear me so I hang up. A half hour later, after I've fallen asleep, the phone rings again.

There she is a second time—now she is in a shop talking to a salesperson. I know this because I hear a lot of French—some good—(the salesperson)—some bad (Nancy).

Again I shout to no avail. This happens at least 3 times a night on every trip and they travel a lot!

The reason this occurs is because, as I am her beloved mother, she has me on automatic redial, so if she reaches into her handbag for anything, my number can inadvertently be touched and viola! I am awakened.

Invariably, she promises to take me off instant redial but so far I am losing a lot of sleep.—

P.S. I really love her a lot.

WHAT I'M LOOKING FORWARD TO

Here it is—the beginning of January 2011, and most of us have high hopes for a wonderful year ahead.

Politically speaking, we want our party of choice to be successful in all endeavors, and we probably all have dreams of a better economy, more jobs for the jobless, more homes for the homeless, friendlier conditions to exist between nations, and in general for America to resume its' former reputation as the leader of the free world.

On a more personal note, I would enjoy fitting into my existing wardrobe without resorting to major alterations, in order to make room for my ever expanding girth.

I would also like to have waiters in the Italian restaurants that I frequent, tell me that pasta has no calories.

I would appreciate being able to remember the names of people I'm supposed to know without having to wonder who the heck they are.

I would also love to have straighter hair while spending the winter in Florida.

It would be most comforting if I were able to find a free parking spot whenever I needed one, so I wouldn't have to have to figure out how to work those new machines that require credit card information.

I would certainly like to be able to finish the New York Times crossword puzzle past Wednesday.

I'm also really looking forward to having my hand held telephones being able to work at all times, without fading away in the middle of a conversation, and thus finding myself talking to myself.

Then too, I would generally like a real person to be on the other end of the phone when I'm calling to report a disaster that may have occurred in one of my appliances.

And if it is at all possible I'd prefer that my blood pressure does not go up in my doctor's office. I don't like him telling me that I have "white coat syndrome". If I *do* have "white coat syndrome" it would be great if he would get another color coat.

Oh—I nearly forgot! The postman! Just when I think I've got real mail, all the envelopes he delivers seem to contain solicitations for money—If I fulfilled *all* these demands I would soon find myself on Medicaid, so—is this what they mean when they say "give till it hurts"? Please Mr. Postman make your request list shorter.

Finally, if all these wonderful New Year innovations will hopefully take place, I would most decidedly like to be a tad younger.

As most of the complaints I've just mentioned are really not good for my old age or blood pressure.

WHAT TO DO

What are average citizens
Like us—supposed to do
Should we believe the Democrats
Or are *G O P* words true?

Should we tax the really rich
Or make cuts on Medicare
No matter which idea we choose
Which one would be most fair?

Who's to say about what's best
To keep our country stable
And is *Congress* or the *President*
The power that's most able?

Is August two the final day?
Will our government stay intact?
Yes! If the guys in Washington
Get off the pot and *ACT!*

AUGUST 23, 2011—
MY EARTHQUAKE

Yesterday I had lunch at Barney's Restaurant in New York with two very dear friends who were my neighbors in Scottsdale, Arizona for twenty winters, and who actually live in Montreal, Canada.

We had a delightful lunch, and after chatting about old times, and then exchanging information about our present lives, we were fast approaching the parting of our ways. They were going to do some New York shopping, and I was going home to Long Island.

Then I decided to call my car service to find out what time their driver would arrive to take me back home and unfortunately I discovered that my cell phone was not working.

Therefore I asked a friendly clerk in one of the Barney's clothing departments if she would place the call for me. She graciously said yes and dialed the number. It would not go through, so I asked if she would mind trying again. She tried a few more times to no avail. She finally said "you don't have the right number". I insisted that I did, but from the look on her face, I believe she thought I was having a senior moment. Sadly I thought she might be right, so I started to look through all the cards in my wallet hoping to find the car service card and possibly see if I *did* have the right number. I could not find the card, and by this time the salesperson, in a rather annoyed tone, suggested that I contact the concierge on the lower floor who might help me find the "correct" telephone number.

Having no other choice, I took the elevator down to the concierge who decided to try my original number—again—no response. But all of a sudden she said "AHA"! Maybe this has something to do with the earthquake—I stupidly asked "what earthquake?" "Oh" she said—"we just got a report that there was a severe earthquake in Brooklyn and that all the bridges are closed—so possibly there is no telephone service".

Much relieved that I probably was *not* "losing it" as they say, I thanked her, and then realized that my car would be delayed because of the bridge closings, therefore I decided to wander around Madison Avenue for a while.

When I got outside I was quite surprised to see many people gathered in front of all the office buildings. I presumed these people were smokers who could not do so in their workplaces, or possibly because it was such a beautiful day, they were just enjoying the lovely weather.

Idiotic Me! I didn't occur to me until much later that they had all been evacuated from their buildings. So there I was right in the middle of my first earthquake and didn't know I was experiencing the effects of it until it was over!

MY HURRICANE

In my mother's day there was a popular song called "goodnight Irene". Now here it is some decades later and I am personally living with another "Irene"—A hurricane!

Four days ago I experienced my first earthquake, and only a few days later here I am nervously expecting the arrival of a very violent hurricane with a possible tornado in the offing as well. What a fearful contemplation!

That's why I am putting pen to paper so that in the future when my descendants discuss their "way back whens", they will comprehend how thrilling and exhilarating my life used to be . . . . ha ha.

Not everybody can undergo two such violent episodes in so short a time, and I therefore consider myself to be unique.

However I have already recovered from my earthquake, but am very much in the midst of my hurricane.

And since I live in a high-rise complex in an area quite near the fast approaching eye of the storm, much preparedness for the event has been necessary.

My terrace furniture is now piled high in my den, my 3 glass tables have been covered with towels, in case the windows that are close to them suddenly blow out. I put several lamps down on the floor so they won't have far to fall, I have plenty of water, food, flashlight and a radio, and hopefully my telephones will work—these things are all within my arm's reach

I also had my hair done yesterday and have my makeup handy if by some chance I am evacuated, as naturally I want to look my best for the neighbors.

But—I forgot to put towels on my window sills, and unfortunately I now have leaks in 2 rooms, my wallpaper in the kitchen is drooping wetly under the window and I am afraid to touch an electric outlet that is quite wet under the kitchen window.

I also stayed in bed all morning because I decided it was the best place to watch the disheartening televised weather news. Those brave windswept and rain drenched newscasters kept up a steady stream of information re: Irene, so I was obligated to, and fascinated by their never ending "on the scene" accounts of the storm.

I also heard about the terrible encroaching of the ocean upon local beaches. In fact the expression the newsmen used was that the ocean was "eating the sand". What an appetite!

Thankfully after several wind howling hours, I am now hearing that things are looking up. Irene is slowly moving North and the few brave souls who endured the violence of the storm, will probably all have pneumonia next week.

News Flash! My lights are still on—the rain is subsiding, and I'm thinking of getting out of bed. Here's to a better tomorrow!

A DEMOCRATIC SOLUTION (BASED ON LYSISTRATA)

I believe I discovered the perfect platform for any new Democratic candidate contemplating a run for the presidency.

It would absolutely outwit every Republican male who wants to repeal Roe V Wade. Let any of those GOPs (who don't want Roe V Wade) promise to repeal it immediately upon becoming president.

But . . . .!!!

Then let every female in America refuse to have sex with any male even her husband!

We would no longer need Roe V Wade because no one would get pregnant and then out of frustration all males would have to accept "gay marriages" as being legal.

It's a win win situation! This would also cut down any increase in population growth and accordingly make for a greener climate.

TITLES OF FORMER BOOKS

1. From Bad To Verse Or the Verse Is Yet To Come

2. If You Take The Train Home Where Do You Put It?

3. Cool Verse And Hot Doggerel

4. At Last Inanimate Objects Speak Up

5. Alphabetical Alliterative Collection Of Corny Compositions

6. "STUFF" From Out Of My Head

Edwards Brothers, Inc.
Thorofare, NJ USA
January 12, 2012